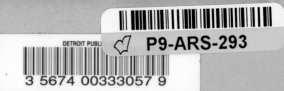

# A TUNE BEYOND US

# A TUNE BEYOND US

*A Collection of Poetry*

*Edited by*

*Myra Cohn Livingston*

ILLUSTRATED BY JAMES J. SPANFELLER

Harcourt, Brace & World, Inc., New York

Library of Congress Catalog Card Number: 68-11502
Printed in the United States of America

First edition

The editor and the publisher thank the following for permis-
sion to reprint the copyrighted material listed below:

AGUILAR, S. A. DE EDICIONES for "La Estrella Venida" and "Con Las
Rosas" by Juan Ramón Jiménez.

GEORGE ALLEN & UNWIN LTD. for "The Adventures of Tom Bombadil"
and "The Stone Troll" from *The Adventures of Tom Bombadil,* and "Dwarves'
Song" from *The Hobbit,* all by J. R. R. Tolkien.

HARRY BEHN for "Gila Monster," "Dragonfly," and "Deer" from *Sombra.*

JONATHAN CAPE LTD. and THE EXECUTORS OF THE JAMES JOYCE ESTATE
for "All day I hear the noise of waters" and the line "I hear an army charging upon the land," both from *Chamber Music* by James Joyce.

CHATTO & WINDUS LTD. for "Go to the Shine That's on a Tree" from *Collected Poems* by Richard Eberhart.

COLLINS-KNOWLTON-WING, INC. for "Dead Cow Farm" by Robert Graves
from *Fairies and Fusiliers,* Copyright © 1918 by Robert Graves.

CONSTABLE AND COMPANY LIMITED for "The Abbot Adam of Angers,"
"Andecavis Abbas," "Easter Sunday," "Carmen Paschale," "Heriger, Bishop
of Mainz," and "Heriger" from *Mediaeval Latin Lyrics,* translated by Helen
Waddell.

CURTIS BROWN, LTD., for "King Tut" from *Nude Descending a Staircase*
by X. J. Kennedy, Copyright © 1961 by X. J. Kennedy.

J. M. DENT & SONS LTD. and the TRUSTEES FOR THE COPYRIGHTS OF THE
LATE DYLAN THOMAS for extracts from "Conversation About Christmas"
by Dylan Thomas.

DODD, MEAD & COMPANY for "Eclogue" and the line ". . . the land where
the bong-tree grows" from *The Complete Nonsense Book* by Edward Lear.

DOUBLEDAY & COMPANY, INC., for "Dinky" and the line "I learn by going
where I have to go" from "The Waking," copyright 1953 by Theodore
Roethke, "The Serpent" and an extract from "Praise to the End," copyright
1950 by Theodore Roethke, "The Minimal," copyright 1942 by Theodore
Roethke, "The Monotony Song," copyright 1955 by Theodore Roethke, an
extract from "The Flight" from "The Lost Son," copyright 1938, 1939 by
Theodore Roethke—all from *Collected Poems of Theodore Roethke*; for
"Loneliness" and "Winter" from *An Introduction to Haiku* by Harold G.
Henderson, Copyright © 1958 by Harold G. Henderson; and for "King Tut,"
copyright © 1961 by X. J. Kennedy, from *Nude Descending a Staircase* by
X. J. Kennedy.

E. P. Dutton & Co., Inc., for "Mrs. Gilfillan" from the book *The Blackbird in the Lilac* by James Reeves, published 1959 by E. P. Dutton; for "Physical Geography" from *Collected Poems* by Louise Townsend Nicholl, Copyright, 1953, by E. P. Dutton & Co., Inc.; and for "What the Gray Cat Sings" from the book *I Sing the Pioneer* by Arthur Guiterman, Copyright, 1926, by E. P. Dutton & Co., Inc., Renewal, 1954, by Mrs. Vida Lindo Guiterman.

Editions du Cloître for "Prière du Papillon," "Prière du Bœuf," and "Prière du Petit Cochon" from *Prières dans l'Arche* by Carmen Bernos de Gasztold, © Editions du Cloître, Limon par Igny, Essonne.

Editorial Losada S. A. for "Canción de Invierno" from *Antolojia Poetica,* 1958; for "Voz Mía" from *Poesia,* 1957; and "A Miss Rápida" from *Eternidades,* 1957 Segunda Edicion, by Juan Ramón Jiménez.

Ann Elmo Agency, Inc., for "Coal for Mike," "Ballad of the Soldier," and "The Mask of Evil" by Bertolt Brecht, translated by H. R. Hays.

James A. Emanuel for "Get Up, Blues," first published in *Phylon,* XXII, No. 1 (Spring 1961) and reprinted in *American Negro Poetry,* edited by Arna Bontemps, Hill & Wang.

Faber and Faber Ltd. for "The Motion of the Earth" from *The Pot Geranium* by Norman Nicholson; for "Buffalo Bill's" from *Selected Poems 1923-1958* by E. E. Cummings; for "Macavity: the Mystery Cat" and "The Song of the Jellicles" from *Old Possum's Book of Practical Cats* by T. S. Eliot; for three lines of "The Dry Salvages" and the line "Home is where one starts from" from "East Coker" from *Four Quartets* by T. S. Eliot used as section titles; for "Dinky," "The Minimal," "The Monotony Song," "The Serpent," extracts from "The Lost Son" and "Praise to the End," and the line "I learn by going where I have to go" from "The Waking," all from *Collected Poems of Theodore Roethke*; for "The Game of Chess" and "The River-Merchant's Wife: A Letter" from *Personae* by Ezra Pound; for "The Brave Man," and for the use of the phrase "A tune beyond us" as the title of this anthology and also for ten lines from "The Man with the Blue Guitar" from *The Collected Poems of Wallace Stevens*; for "Beethoven's Death Mask" from *Collected Poems* by Stephen Spender; for extracts from "Sext" from *Collected Shorter Poems 1927-1957* by W. H. Auden; and for the line "... imaginary gardens with real toads" from "Poetry" from *Collected Poems of Marianne Moore.*

Farrar, Straus and Giroux, Inc., for "The Coming Star," "My Voice," "To Miss Rápida," "Winter Song," and "With the Roses" from *Selected Writings of Juan Ramón Jiménez,* translated by H. R. Hays, Copyright © 1957 by Juan Ramón Jiménez.

Julia Fields for "Madness One Monday Evening" from *New Negro Poets: U.S.A.,* Indiana University Press.

Grove Press, Inc., for "Artichoke," "Oda a la Alcachofa," "Diver," "Oda al Buzo," and extracts from "A Few Things Explained" and "Explicio Algunas Cosas," all from *Selected Poems of Pablo Neruda,* edited and translated by Ben Belitt, Copyright © 1961 by Grove Press, Inc.; for "Bicycles" from *Selected Poems of Andrei Voznesensky,* translated and with an introduction by Anselm Hollo, Copyright © 1964 by Grove Press, Inc.

Harcourt, Brace & World, Inc., for "Buffalo Bill's" and "hist whist" from *Poems 1923-1954,* Copyright, 1923, 1951, by E. E. Cummings; for "porky and porkie" from *Poems 1923-1954,* Copyright, 1938, by E. E. Cummings, renewed, 1966, by Marion Morehouse Cummings; for the line "Home is where one starts from" from "East Coker" and three lines from "Dry Salvages," used as section titles, from *Four Quartets* by T. S. Eliot; for

English Opera," "The Elephant, or the Force of Habit," "Away with blood-shed," "As I was walking slowly," and "Amelia mixed the mustard"; as the literary representative of the Estate of the late James Joyce for "All day I hear the noise of waters," "On the Beach at Fontana," and the line "I hear an army charging upon the land."

STEPHEN SPENDER for translations of "The Lizard Is Crying" and "Ballad of the Little Square" by Federico García Lorca.

UNIVERSITY OF CALIFORNIA PRESS for "The Little Trumpet" by Corrado Govoni, translated by Carlo L. Golino; and an extract from "You Were Shattered" by Giuseppe Ungaretti, translated by Lowry Nelson, Jr., from *Contemporary Italian Poetry* edited by Carlo L. Golino.

THE VIKING PRESS, INC., for "The Prayer of the Butterfly," "The Prayer of the Little Pig," and "The Prayer of the Ox" from *Prayers from the Ark* by Carmen Bernos de Gasztold, translated by Rumer Godden, Copyright © 1962 by Rumer Godden; for "All day I hear the noise of waters" and the line "I hear an army charging upon the land" from *Collected Poems* by James Joyce, Copyright 1918 by B. W. Huebsch, Inc., 1946 by Nora Joyce; for "On the Beach at Fontana" from *Collected Poems* by James Joyce, Copyright 1927 by James Joyce, All rights reserved.

OSBORNE WARD as administrators of the estate of the late Lady Strachie for "Eclogue" and the line ". . . the land where the bong-tree grows" from *The Complete Nonsense Book* by Edward Lear.

A. P. WATT & SON, MR. M. B. YEATS, and MACMILLAN & CO. LTD. (LONDON) for "Anashuya and Vijaya," "Fergus and the Druid," "The Host of the Air," "The Cat and the Moon," "The Old Men Admiring Themselves in the Water," and the line "Come away, O human child!" from "The Stolen Child," all from *Collected Poems of W. B. Yeats.*

A. P. WATT & SON and MISS D. E. COLLINS for "In the Evening" from *The Coloured Lands* by G. K. Chesterton.

A. P. WATT & SON and ROBERT GRAVES for "Dead Cow Farm" from *Fairies and Fusiliers* by Robert Graves.

WEIDENFELD & NICOLSON LIMITED for "Brooklyn Bridge" from *The Bedbug and Selected Poetry* by Vladimir Mayakovsky, edited by Patricia Blake and translated by Max Hayward and George Reavey.

WESLEYAN UNIVERSITY PRESS for "The Cradle Trap" from *At the End of the Open Road* by Louis Simpson, Copyright © 1961 by Louis Simpson.

THE WORLD PUBLISHING COMPANY for the English and Russian texts of "Brooklyn Bridge" from *The Bedbug and Selected Poetry* by Vladimir M. Mayakovsky, edited by Patricia Blake, translated by George Reavey and Max Hayward, Copyright © 1960 by The World Publishing Company.

The editor and the publisher have made every effort to locate all holders of copyright and would be glad to hear from anyone not reached.

The editor wishes to express appreciation to Tamara Chapro for assistance with the poems in the Russian language.

*To Josh and Jonas*

The man bent over his guitar,
A shearsman of sorts. The day was green.

They said, "You have a blue guitar,
You do not play things as they are."

The man replied, "Things as they are,
Are changed upon the blue guitar."

And they said then, "But play you must
A tune beyond us, yet ourselves,

A tune upon the blue guitar
Of things exactly as they are."

Wallace Stevens

*from "The Man with the Blue Guitar"*

# EDITOR'S NOTE

Every poem in this collection will not speak for you.
But perhaps one, or two, will.
And that will be enough.

A particular poem is not for everybody. It is for that person who reads or listens to it, finding in its words something that appeals to him—meeting laughter or wonder or a way of looking at the world that expresses his own way of seeing and hearing and feeling. When such a poem is found, so also is the poet, for the poet is an individual who feels so deeply about his world that he must tell others about it. And he does this in the way he knows best, through words and music and rhythms.

Here are poems flung in time from eighth-century China to present-day Italy or Alabama. Written in many languages, they are presented that those who read other languages may enjoy the music of the original, as well as the English translation. Here are silly, nonsensical rhymes; tunes "beyond us"; poems for two voices to be read aloud with friends; poems in established forms of pattern and rhyme or the more contemporary idiom; poems occasionally unfinished or in fragments.

Not many of these poems will be familiar. Poems best known are to be found in other anthologies. This collection has been chosen, largely, from the lesser known works of great poets or from the work of little-known poets: a German who tells of a railroad man in Ohio, an Irishman who sees the Devil, a Latin poet of the ninth century writing of Easter Sunday, a Russian marveling at the Brooklyn Bridge, poets of Spain, China,

England, and America observing the tragedies of war, a Chilean poet looking at a deep-sea diver, a Welshman remembering Christmas, a French poet imagining the feelings of animals, an American speaking of flying saucers.

In an age of science and definition, it sometimes seems important to reflect that art escapes definition by its appeal to man's senses, sensitivities, and emotions. Poetry is a place where we are not expected to define or analyze or answer questions. We can simply laugh or cry or wonder—or turn the page until we find a poem that sings the tune we wish to hear. It's as easy as that.

# CONTENTS

# A TUNE BEYOND US

''Home is where one starts from . . .''

T. S. ELIOT

# *From* ON A BICYCLE

YEVGENY YEVTUSHENKO

*Translated by Robin Milner-Gulland and Peter Levi, S. J.*

Under the dawn I wake my two-wheel friend.
Shouting in bed my mother says to me,
"Mind you don't clatter it going downstairs!"
I walk him down he springing step to step:
those tyres he has, if you pat him flat-handed
he'll bounce your hand. I mount with an air
and as light a pair of legs as you'll encounter,
slow into Sunday ride out of the gates,
roll along asphalt, press down on the pedals,
speeding,                    fearless,
          ring,
               ring,
                    ring

                    .    .    .

Flinging along my happiness my fever,
incapable of breaking out of it,
overtaking the lorries on the road
taking each of them in a single swoop
flying behind them through cut open space
hanging on them uphill. Yes I know.
It's dangerous. I enjoy it. They hoot
and lean out and yell out,
"We'll give you a hand on the hills;
give you some speed; after that
you tear along on your own."
Careering full tilt, pelting along
in a flurry of jokes. Turn a blind eye
to my crazy career; it's the fashion.
You can't tell me how terribly I ride.
One day I'll learn how to ride.

19

ЕВГЕНИЙ ЕВТУШЕНКО

Я бужу на заре
своего двухколёсного друга.
Мать кричит из постели:
« На леснице хоть не трезвонь! »
Я свожу его вниз.
По ступеням

        он скачет

                упруго.

Стукнуть шину ладонью—
и сразу подскочит ладонь!
Я небрежно сажусь—
Вы посадки такой не видали!
Из ворот выезжаю
навстречу воскресному дню.
Я качу по асфальту.
Я весело жму на педали.
Я бесстрашно гоню,
и звоню,

        и звоню,

             и звоню . . .

Я качу!
Не могу я с весёлостью прущей расстаться.
Грузовые в пути
догоняю я махом одним.
Я за ними лечу
в разрежённом пространстве.
На подъёмах крутых
прицепляюсь я к ним.
Знаю сам, что опасно!
Люблю я рискованность!
Говорят мне,

гудя напряжённо,
                они:
« На подъёме поможем,
дадим тебе скорость,
ну, а дальше уже,
как сумеешь, гони. »
Я гоню что есть мочи!
Я шутками лихо кидаюсь.
Только вы не глядите,
как шало я мчусь,—
это так, для фасону,
я знаю, что плохо катаюсь.
Но когда-нибудь
я хорошо научусь.

# FRAGMENT OF AN ENGLISH OPERA
(Designed as a model for young librettists)

A. E. HOUSMAN

*Dramatis personae:*
Father (bass)
Mother (contralto)
Daughter (soprano)

*Scene:* a Room　　*Time:* Evening

*Father:*　　Retire, my daughter;
　　　　　　Prayers have been said;
　　　　　Take your warm water
　　　　　And go to bed.

*Daughter:*　But I had rather
　　　　　Sit up instead.

*Father:*　　I am your father,
　　　　　So go to bed.

*Daughter:*　Are you my father?

*Father:*　　I think so, rather:
　　　　　You go to bed.


*Mother:*　　My daughter, vanish;
　　　　　You hear me speak:
　　　　　This is not Spanish,
　　　　　Nor is it Greek.

*Daughter:*　Oh, what a bother!
　　　　　Would I were dead!

*Mother:*　　I am your mother,
　　　　　So go to bed.

*Daughter:*　Are you my mother?

*Mother:*　　You have no other:
　　　　　You go to bed.

| | |
|---|---|
| *Father:* | Take your bed-candle<br>   And take it quick.<br>This is the handle. |
| *Daughter:* | Is *this* the handle? |
| *Father:* |    No, that's the wick.<br>*This* is the handle,<br>   At this end here.<br>Take your bed-candle<br>   And disappear. |
| *Daughter:* | Oh dear, oh dear! |
| *Father & Mother:* | Take your warm water,<br>   As we have said;<br>You are our daughter,<br>   So go to bed. |
| *Daughter:* | Am I your daughter? |
| *Father & Mother:* | If not, you oughter:<br>   You go to bed. |
| | |
| *Daughter:* | I am their daughter;<br>If not, I oughter:<br>   Prayers have been said.<br>This is my mother;<br>I have no other:<br>   Would I were dead!<br>That is my father;<br>He thinks so, rather:<br>   Oh dear, oh dear!<br>I take my candle;<br>*This* is the handle:<br>   I disappear. |
| *Father & Mother:* |    The coast is clear. |

# THIS IS JUST TO SAY

WILLIAM CARLOS WILLIAMS

I have eaten
the plums
that were in
the icebox

and which
you were probably
saving
for breakfast

Forgive me
they were delicious
so sweet
and so cold


## *From* SONGS FROM AN ISLAND
## IN THE MOON

WILLIAM BLAKE

XII

O, I say, you Joe,
Throw us the ball!
I've a good mind to go
And leave you all.
I never saw such a bowler
To bowl the ball in a tansy,

And to clean it with my hankercher
Without saying a word.

That Bill's a foolish fellow;
He has given me a black eye.
He does not know how to handle a bat
Any more than a dog or a cat:
He has knock'd down the wicket,
And broke the stumps,
And runs without shoes to save his pumps.


*From* THE LOST WORLD

## I. CHILDREN'S ARMS

RANDALL JARRELL

                        . . . and I
See on the back seat (sight more appealing
Than any human sight!) my own friend Lucky,
Half wolf, half police-dog. And he can play the piano—
Play that he does, that is—and jump so high
For a ball that he turns a somersault. "Hello,"
I say to the lady, and hug Lucky . . . In my
Talk with the world, in which it tells me what I
   know
And I tell it, "I know—" how strange that I
Know nothing, and yet it tells me what I know!—
I appreciate the animals, who stand by
Purring. Or else they sit and pant. It's so—
So *agreeable*. If only people purred and panted!

# POEM

LANGSTON HUGHES

I loved my friend.
He went away from me.
There's nothing more to say.
The poem ends,
Soft as it began—
I loved my friend.

# LOCKED OUT

## AS TOLD TO A CHILD

ROBERT FROST

When we locked up the house at night,
We always locked the flowers outside
And cut them off from window light.
The time I dreamed the door was tried
And brushed with buttons upon sleeves,
The flowers were out there with the thieves.
Yet nobody molested them!
We did find one nasturtium
Upon the steps with bitten stem.
I may have been to blame for that:
I always thought it must have been
Some flower I played with as I sat
At dusk to watch the moon down early.


## *From* ZIMA JUNCTION

YEVGENY YEVTUSHENKO

*Translated by Robin Milner-Gulland and Peter Levi, S. J.*

I sat beneath a birch, beneath an oak,
so many meditations
                    thought of you
Uncle Volodya, Uncle Andrei,
with love.

31

Andrei's the elder
I love his sleeping, crumpled,
                                 hardly living,
the way he washes, rising very early,
the way he carries other people's children.
He runs the garage, everlastingly
enraged and smeared all over, careers
along in a van he calls the Billygoat,
with his big forehead hunched over the wheel.
His sudden quarrels, disappearances
into the country for a day or two,
and home he comes, benevolent and tired,
smelling of petrol and of virgin forest.
He likes to shake a hand until it cracks,
in fights he throws people around by twos
for amusement, does everything gaily and well,
from wood-cutting to sprinkling salt on bread.
Uncle Volodya: wonderful
the working metal seems as he grips it
shaking the woodshavings out of his hair,
and ankle-deep in the light-coloured foam:
and there's a carpenter! A carpenter!
and what a storyteller, an expert,
and often standing in the barn or sitting
on one side perched up on his joiner's bench
—about the cook who stole and who was shot
and how the fighters passed through a village
and Francesca the woman who came
from Petersburg sang the song to them.

Oh my uncles.

# COBB WOULD HAVE CAUGHT IT

ROBERT FITZGERALD

In sunburnt parks where Sundays lie,
Or the wide wastes beyond the cities,
Teams in grey deploy through sunlight.

Talk it up boys, a little practice.

Coming in stubby and fast, the baseman
Gathers a grounder in fat green grass,
Picks it stinging and clipped as wit
Into the leather: a swinging step
Wings it deadeye down to first.
Smack. Oh, attaboy, attyoldboy.

Catcher reverses his cap, pulls down
Sweaty casque, and squats in the dust:
Pitcher rubs new ball on his pants,
Chewing, puts a jet behind him;
Nods past batter, taking his time.
Batter settles, tugs at his cap:
A spinning ball: step and swing to it,
Caught like a cheek before it ducks
By shivery hickory: socko, baby:
Cleats dig into the dust. Outfielder,
On his way, looking over shoulder,
Makes it a triple. A long peg home.

Innings and afternoons. Fly lost in sunset.
Throwing arm gone bad. There's your old ball game.
Cool reek of the field. Reek of companions.

# *From* CONVERSATION ABOUT CHRISTMAS

... after dinner

DYLAN THOMAS

The Uncles sat in front of the fire, took off their collars, loosened all buttons, put their large moist hands over their watch-chains, groaned a little, and slept. Mothers, aunts, and sisters scuttled to and fro, bearing tureens. The dog was sick. Auntie Beattie had to have three aspirins, but Auntie Hannah, who liked port, stood in the middle of the snowbound back-yard, singing like a big-bosomed thrush. I would blow up balloons to see how big they would blow up to; and, when they burst, which they all did, the Uncles jumped and rumbled. In the rich and heavy afternoon, the Uncles breathing like dolphins and the snow descending, I would sit in the front room, among festoons and Chinese lanterns, and nibble at dates, and try to make a model man-o'-war, following the Instructions for Little Engineers, and produce what might be mistaken for a sea-going tram. And then, at Christmas tea, the recovered Uncles would be jolly over their mince-pies; and the great iced cake loomed in the centre of the table like a marble grave. Auntie Hannah laced her tea with rum, because it was only once a year. And in the evening, there was Music. An uncle played the fiddle, a cousin sang Cherry Ripe, and another uncle sang Drake's Drum. It was very warm in the little house. Auntie Hannah, who had got on to the parsnip wine, sang a song about Rejected Love, and Bleeding Hearts, and Death, and then another in which she said that her Heart was like a Bird's Nest; and then everybody laughed again, and then I went to bed. Looking through my bedroom window, out into the moonlight and the flying, unending, smoke-coloured snow, I could see the lights in the windows of all the other houses on our hill, and hear the music rising from them up the long, steadily falling night. I turned the gas down, I got into bed. I said some words to the close and holy darkness, and then I slept.

# PHYSICAL GEOGRAPHY

LOUISE TOWNSEND NICHOLL

Sudden refreshment came upon the school
When in the tired afternoon we read
Of Rainfall, mountain ranges, watershed.
The whole United States stretched wide and cool.
Geography was dull; this other kind
With gulfs and glaciers, caves, and Rock Formation
In place of Products, People, Population,
Diffused a thrilling vapor through the mind.

There were three creatures—water, land and air—
Shifting so lightly yet with deep intent
Over the Country and the Continent,
Great creatures moving somber and aware,
Mixing and changing, making something new.
Theirs was the only work that never stops—
More interesting than Industries and Crops—
Creating clouds and sand and snow and dew.

And they could fashion terror when they listed:
New words like "funnel," "vortex," "spiral motion"
Explained the fearful Storms on Plains and Ocean.
Our dreams were sucked up violently and twisted,
The walls and blackboards slowly curved and spun,
There was a revolving speed, a rising core.
This room would not confine us as before
Since cyclones and tornadoes had begun.

# FISHING FOR SNAKES

RICHARD EBERHART

Fishing for snakes
In the wide well of summertime
Depends upon the kind of rake
Best nets their slidy shine.

They will slip a butterfly net,
Which is too delicate, unsubtle,
But if persistent you can catch them yet,
On your belly in a downward effort.

It is an extension of the hand
In the rake like a fan, and firm,
Wide, with fingers in a fixed half clench
Will sweep the well and fault their swim.

It is all a kind of trick,
Obscured in method, but never despair.
After exertion, with a certain flick,
You can fling them up in the air.

I don't say that I would kill one,
Although this is nothing to shun,
But I like to see the fellows run,
Wriggling away in an evil sun.

"... every atom belonging to me ..."

WALT  WHITMAN

# *From* CONVERSATION ABOUT CHRISTMAS
## ... the Useful Presents ...

DYLAN THOMAS

There were the Useful Presents: engulfing mufflers of the old coach days, and mittens made for giant sloths; zebra scarves of a substance like silky gum that could be tug-o'-warred down to the goloshes; blinding tam-o'-shanters like patchwork tea cosies and bunny-scutted busbies and balaclavas for victims of head-shrinking tribes; from aunts who always wore wool next to the skin there were mustached and rasping vests that made you wonder why the aunties had any skin left at all; and once I had a little crocheted nose bag from an aunt now, alas, no longer whinnying with us. And pictureless books in which small boys, though warned with quotations, not to, *would* skate on Farmer Garge's pond and did, and drowned; and books that told me everything about the wasp, except why.

DYLAN THOMAS

Of course there were sweets. It was the marshmallows that squelched. Hardboileds, toffee, fudge and allsorts, crunches, cracknels, humbugs, glaciers, and marzipan and butterwelsh for the Welsh. And troops of bright tin soldiers who, if they would not fight, could always run. And Snakes-and-Families and Happy Ladders. And Easy Hobbi-Games for Little Engineers, complete with Instructions. Oh, easy for Leonardo! And a whistle to make the dogs bark to wake up the old man next door to make him beat on the wall with his stick to shake our picture off the wall. And a packet of cigarettes: you put one in your mouth and you stood at the corner of the street and you waited for hours, in vain, for an old lady to scold you for smoking a cigarette and then, with a smirk, you ate it. And, last of all, in the toe of the stocking, sixpence like a silver corn.

# THE CHING-TING MOUNTAIN

LI PO

*Translated by Shigeyoshi Obata*

Flocks of birds have flown high and away;
A solitary drift of cloud, too, has gone, wandering on.
And I sit alone with the Ching-ting Peak, towering beyond.
We never grow tired of each other, the mountain and I.

只有敬亭山。　　衆鳥高飛盡。孤雲獨去閑。　　獨坐敬亭山。相看兩不厭。

李白

# BICYCLES

ANDREI  VOZNESENSKY

*Translated by Anselm Hollo*

The bicycles lie
In the woods, in the dew.
    Between the birch trees
    The highroad gleams.

They fell, fell down
Mudguard to mudguard,
    Handlebar to handlebar
    Pedal to pedal.

And you can't
Wake them up!
    Petrified monsters,
    Their chains entwined.

Huge and surprised
They stare at the sky.
    Above them, green dusk
    Resin, and bumblebees.

In the luxurious
Rustling of camomile, peppermint
    Leaves they lie, Forgotten,
    Asleep. Asleep.

# ЛЕЖАТ ВЕЛОСИПЕДЫ...

АНДРЕЙ ВОЗНЕСЕНСКИЙ

Лежат велосипеды
в лесу в росе
в березовых просветах
блестит шоссе

попадали припали
крылом—к крылу
педалями—в педали
рулём—к рулю

да разве их разбудишь—
ну хоть убей!—
оцепенелых чудищ
в витках цепей

большие изумленные
глядят с земли
над ними—мгла зеленая
смола
    шмели

в шумящем изобилии
ромашек мят
лежат
о них забыли
и спят
    и спят

# THE GAME OF CHESS

## DOGMATIC STATEMENT CONCERNING THE GAME OF CHESS: THEME FOR A SERIES OF PICTURES

EZRA POUND

Red knights, brown bishops, bright queens,
Striking the board, falling in strong "L"s of
      colour.
Reaching and striking in angles,
          holding lines in one colour.
This board is alive with light;
          these pieces are living in form,
Their moves break and reform the pattern:
          luminous green from the rocks,
Clashing with "X"s of queens,
          looped with the knight-leaps.

"Y" pawns, cleaving, embanking!
Whirl! Centripetal! Mate! King down in the
      vortex,
Clash, leaping of bands, straight strips of hard
      colour,
Blocked lights working in. Escapes. Renewal of
      contest.

# THE STARFISH

ROBERT P. TRISTRAM COFFIN

Triangles are commands of God
   And independent lie
Outside our brains as wild geese show
   Travelling down the sky.

And this five-pointed thing that sucks
   Its slow way as it can
Has as sure a hold on God
   As great Aldebaran.

It has as large a power to please
   Any eye that gazes
Upon its harmony of lines
   As ancient Attic vases.

Pentagon for Gawain's shield,
   Five points of chivalry,
In ancient laws and musical
   It creeps below the sea.

Its fingers are on God's own hand,
   Its just name is a star,
Through aeons it remains as right
   As birth and dying are.

# ON THE GIFT OF A CLOAK

HUGO OF ORLEANS, KNOWN AS PRIMAS
*Translated by George F. Whicher*

*Primas*

Scum of clergymen! clergy's dregs!
Pain i' the neck, who gave me
An unlined cloak to save me
From winter's cold, i' fegs!

*Bystander*

Who was it then presented
This—shall we say—integument?
It wasn't bought or rented?
It's yours?

*Primas*

Yes, mine; I meant
Merely to say I mind it
That he who gave it tore away what lined it.

*Bystander*

But who then was the donor?

*Primas*

A certain prelate gave it me—the owner.

*Bystander*

*He* gave this gift so proud!
He might as well have given you a shroud.
For service in all weathers
What good's a cloak with neither fur nor feathers?
You'll see, when snow is driving,
You'll catch your death of cold—there's no surviving.

## Primas

Poor mantle, what abuse could thin you?
No fur, no padding in you!
Think you, thus sadly aging,
To fend me from the blast, the storm's mad raging,
To shield me and protect me
So piercing cold will not affect me,
That in your keeping surely
I may withstand the wintry winds securely?

## The Mantle thus responded:

No pelt, no fleece is left, my fur's absconded;
Worn smooth am I, and like a head bare
My texture's threadbare.
The biting north to chill you
Will drive his lances through me fit to kill you.
There's no escaping
The wind's assault while all these holes are gaping;
A thousand vents in each direction
Will strip you of protection.

## Primas

You think we're in for freezing?

## The Mantle

I do, and you with cold are wheezing.
But till some fur is added,
It's little help you'll get from me, unpadded.
Know what, Primas? I together
With peltries could repel this pelting weather;
Buy furs, and thus augmented
I'll fight the storm and keep you well contented.
Your plight I pity truly
And if I could, would help you duly,
But when it comes to hair my make-up
Is less like Esau than like Jacob.

45

# PONTIFICUM SPUMA

PRIMAS

Pontificum spuma, fex cleri, sordida struma,
qui dedit in bruma michi mantellum sine pluma!

—Hoc indumentum tibi quis dedit? an fuit emptum?
estne tuum?

　　　　　　　—Nostrum; sed qui dedit, abstulit ostrum.

—Quis dedit hoc munus?

　　　　　　　　　—Presul michi prebuit unus.

—Qui dedit hoc munus, dedit hoc in munere funus.
Quid valet in bruma clamis absque pilo, sine pluma?
Cernis adesse nives: moriere gelu neque vives.

—Pauper mantelle, macer absque pilo, sine pelle,
si potes, expelle boream rabiemque procelle!
Sis michi pro scuto, ne frigore pungar acuto!
Per te posse puto ventis obsistere tuto.

Tunc ita mantellus:—Michi nec pilus est neque vellus.
Sum levis absque pilo, tenui sine tegmine filo.
Te mordax aquilo per me feriet quasi pilo.
Si notus iratus patulos perflabit hiatus,
stringet utrumque latus per mille foramina flatus.

—Frigus adesse vides?

　　　　　　　　—Video, quia frigore strides:
sed michi nulla fides, nisi pelliculas clamidi des.
Scis, quid ages, Primas? eme pelles, obstrue rimas!
Tunc bene depellam, iuncta michi pelle procellam.
Conpatior certe, moveor pietate super te
et facerem iussum, sed Iacob non Esau sum.

# GO FLY A SAUCER

DAVID McCORD

I've seen one flying saucer. Only when
It flew across our sight in 1910
We little thought about the little men.

But let's suppose the little men were there
To cozy such a disc through foreign air:
Connecticut was dark, but didn't scare.

I wonder what they thought of us, and why
They chose the lesser part of Halley's sky,
And went away and let the years go by

Without return? Or did they not get back
To Mars or Venus through the cosmic flak?
At least they vanished, every spaceman Jack.

Now they are with us in the books, in air,
In argument, in hope, in fear, in spare
Reports from men aloft who saw them there.

The day one saucer cracks, the greatest egg
Since dinosaur and dodo shook a leg
Will give new meaning to the prefix *meg*.

Some say the saucers with their little race
Of little men from Littlesphere in space
Have sensed our international disgrace.

And when the thing blows over, up, or what,
They'll gladly land and give us all they've got
So Earth shall cease to be a trouble spot.

One fact as old as Chaucer, Saucer Men:
You may be little as a bantam hen,
But Earth has specialized in little men.


# THE LITTLE TRUMPET

CORRADO GOVONI

*Translated by Carlo L. Golino*

All that is left
of the magic of the fair
is this little trumpet
of blue and green tin,
blown by a girl
as she walks, barefoot, through the fields.
But within its forced note
are all the clowns, white ones and red ones,
the band all dressed in gaudy gold,
the merry-go-round, the calliope, the lights.
Just as in the dripping of the gutter
is all the fearfulness of the storm
the beauty of lightning and the rainbow;
and in the damp flickers of a firefly
whose light dissolves on a heather branch
is all the wondrousness of spring.

# LA TROMBETTINA

CORRADO GOVONI

Ecco che cosa resta
di tutta la magia della fiera:
quella trombettina,
di latta azzurra e verde,
che suona una bambina
camminando, scalza, per i campi.
Ma, in quella nota sforzata,
ci sono dentro i pagliacci bianchi e rossi,
c'è la banda d'oro rumoroso,
la giostra coi cavalli, l'organo, i lumini.
Come, nel sgocciolare della gronda,
c'è tutto lo spavento della bufera,
la bellezza dei lampi e dell'arcobaleno;
nell'umido cerino d'una lucciola
che si sfa su una foglia di brughiera,
tutta la meraviglia della primavera.


# THE CAROUSEL
## JARDIN DU LUXEMBOURG

RAINER MARIA RILKE
*Translated by M. D. Herter Norton*

With a roof and its shadow it rotates
a little while, the herd of particolored
horses, all from the land
that lingers long ere it sinks out of sight.
Some it is true are hitched to carriages,

yet all of them have mettle in their mien;
a vicious red lion goes with them
and every now and then a white elephant.

Even a deer is there quite as in the woods,
save that he bears a saddle and on that
a little blue girl buckled up.

And on the lion rides all white a boy
and holds himself with his small hot hand,
the while the lion shows his teeth and tongue.

And every now and then a white elephant.

And on the horses they come passing by,
girls too, bright girls, who almost have outgrown
this leap of horses; midway in their swing
they look up, anywhere, across—

And every now and then a white elephant.

And this goes on and hurries that it may end,
and only circles and turns and has no goal.
A red, a green, a gray being sent by,
some little profile hardly yet begun.
And occasionally a smile, turning this way,
a happy one, that dazzles and dissipates
over this blind and breathless game.

# DAS KARUSSELL

## JARDIN DU LUXEMBOURG

RAINER MARIA RILKE

Mit einem Dach und seinem Schatten dreht
sich eine kleine Weile der Bestand
von bunten Pferden, alle aus dem Land,
das lange zögert, eh es untergeht.
Zwar manche sind an Wagen angespannt,
doch alle haben Mut in ihren Mienen;
ein böser roter Löwe geht mit ihnen
und dann und wann ein weisser Elefant.

Sogar ein Hirsch ist da ganz wie im Wald,
nur dass er einen Sattel trägt und drüber
ein kleines blaues Mädchen aufgeschnallt.

Und auf dem Löwen reitet weiss ein Junge
und halt sich mit der kleinen heissen Hand,
dieweil der Löwe Zähne zeigt und Zunge.

Und dann und wann ein weisser Elefant.

Und auf den Pferden kommen sie vorüber,
auch Mädchen, helle, diesem Pferdesprunge
fast schon entwachsen; mitten in dem Schwunge
schauen sie auf, irgendwohin, herüber—

Und dann und wann ein weisser Elefant.

Und das geht hin und eilt sich, dass es endet,
und kreist und dreht sich nur und hat kein Ziel.
Ein Rot, ein Grün, ein Grau vorbeigesendet,
ein kleines kaum begonnenes Profil.

Und manchesmal ein Lächeln, hergewendet,
ein seliges, das blendet und verschwendet
an dieses atemlose blinde Spiel.


## A BOY LOOKING AT BIG DAVID

MAY SWENSON

I'm touching his toe.
I know I'll be brave after this.
His toenail wide as my hand,
I have to stand tall to reach it.

The big loose hand with the rock in it
by his thigh
is high above my head. The vein
from wrist to thumb, a blue strain in the marble.

As if it had natural anatomy all its own
inside it.
Somebody skinned off the top stone,
and there He stands.

I'd like to climb up there on that slippery Hip,
shinny up to the Shoulder
the other side of that thumping Neck,
and lie in the ledge on the collar-bone,

by the sling.
In that cool place
I'd stare-worship that big, full-lipped,
frown-browned, far-eyed, I-dare-you-Face.

I'd like to live on that David for a while,
get to know
how to be immortal like Him.
But I can only reach his Toe—

broad, poking over the edge of the stand.
So cool . . .
Maybe, marble Him,
he likes the warm of my hand?


# ARTICHOKE

PABLO NERUDA
*Translated by Ben Belitt*

The artichoke
of delicate heart
erect
in its battle-dress, builds
its minimal cupola;
keeps
stark
in its scallop of
scales.
Around it,
demoniac vegetables
bristle their thicknesses,
devise
tendrils and belfries,
the bulb's agitations;
while under the subsoil

the carrot
sleeps sound in its
rusty mustaches.
Runner and filaments
bleach in the vineyards,
whereon rise the vines.
The sedulous cabbage
arranges
its petticoats;
oregano
sweetens a world;
and the artichoke
dulcetly there in a gardenplot,
armed for a skirmish,
goes proud
in its pomegranate
burnishes.
Till, on a day,
each by the other,
the artichoke moves
to its dream
of a market place
in the big willow
hoppers:
a battle formation.
Most warlike
of defilades—
with men
in the market stalls,
white shirts
in the soup-greens,
artichoke
field marshals,
close-order conclaves,
commands, detonations,

and voices,
a crashing of crate staves.

And
Maria
come
down
with her hamper
to
make trial
of an artichoke:
she reflects, she examines,
she candles them up to the light like an egg,
never flinching;
she bargains,
she tumbles her prize
in a market bag
among shoes and a
cabbage head,
a bottle
of vinegar; is back
in her kitchen.
The artichoke drowns in an olla.

So you have it:
a vegetable, armed,
a profession
(call it an artichoke)
whose end
is millennial.
We taste of that
sweetness,
dismembering
scale after scale.

We eat of a halcyon paste:
it is green at the artichoke heart.


## ODA A LA ALCACHOFA

PABLO NERUDA

La alcachofa
de tierno corazón
se vistió de guerrero,
erecta, construyó
una pequeña cúpula,
se mantuvo
impermeable
bajo
sus escamas,
a su lado
los vegetables locos
se encresparon,
se hicieron
zarcillos, espadañas,
bulbos conmovedores,
en el subsuelo
durmió la zanahoria
de bigotes rojos,
la viña
resecó los sarmientos
por donde sube el vino,
la col
se dedicó
a probarse faldas,
el orégano

a perfumar el mundo,
y la dulce
alcachofa
allí en el huerto,
vestida de guerrero,
bruñida
como una granada,
orgullosa;
y un día
una con otra
en grandes cestos
de mimbre, caminó
por el mercado
a realizar su sueño:
la milicia.
En hileras
nunca fué tan marcial
como en la feria,
los hombres
entre las legumbres
con sus camisas blancas
eran
mariscales
de las alcachofas,
las filas apretadas,
las voces de comando,
y la detonación
de una caja que cae;

pero
entonces
viene
María
con su cesto,
escoge

una alcachofa,
no le teme,
la examina, la observa
contra la luz como si fuera un huevo,
la compra,
la confunde
en su bolsa
con un par de zapatos,
con un repollo y una
botella
de vinagre
hasta
que entrando a la cocina
la sumerge en la olla.

Así termina
en paz
esta carrera
.del vegetal armado
que se llama alcachofa,
luego
escama por escama,
desvestimos
la delicia
ya comemos
la pacífica pasta
de su corazón verde.

'' . . . the land where the bong-tree grows''

EDWARD LEAR

# KING TUT

X. J. KENNEDY

King Tut
Crossed over the Nile
On steppingstones of crocodile.

*King Tut!*
His mother said,
*Come here this minute!*
*You'll get wet feet.*
King Tut is dead

And now King Tut
Tight as a nut
Keeps his big fat Mummy shut.

King Tut,
      tut, tut.

A. E. HOUSMAN

Amelia mixed the mustard,
  She mixed it good and thick;
She put it in the custard
  And made her Mother sick,
And showing satisfaction
  By many a loud huzza
"Observe" said she "the action
  Of mustard on Mamma."

# THE PRAYER OF THE LITTLE PIG

CARMEN BERNOS DE GASZTOLD

*Translated by Rumer Godden*

Lord,
their politeness makes me laugh!
Yes, I grunt!
Grunt and snuffle!
I grunt because I grunt
and snuffle
because I cannot do anything else!
All the same, I am not going to thank them
for fattening me up to make bacon.
Why did You make me so tender?
What a fate!
Lord,
Teach me how to say

Amen

# PRIÈRE DU PETIT COCHON

CARMEN BERNOS DE GASZTOLD

Seigneur,
ils me font rire avec leur politesse!
Oui, je grogne!
Je grogne et je renifle!
Je grogne parce, que je grogne!
Et je renifle,

parce que je ne peux pas faire autrement!
Je ne vais tout de même pas les remercier
de m'engraisser pour leur saloir?
Pourquoi m'avez-Vous fait si tendre?
Quelle destinée!
Seigneur,
apprenez-moi à dire:
        Ainsi soit-il!


## THE MONOTONY SONG

THEODORE ROETHKE

A donkey's tail is very nice
You musn't pull it more than twice,
Now there's a piece of good advice
  —Heigho, meet Hugh and Harry!

One day Hugh walked up to a bear
And said, Old Boy, you're shedding hair,
And shedding more than here and there,
  —Heigho, we're Hugh and Harry!

The bear said, Sir, you go too far,
I wonder who you think you are
To make remarks about my—Grrrr!
  —And there was only Harry!

This Harry ran straight up a wall,
But found he wasn't there at all,
And so he had a horrid fall.
  —Alas, alack for Harry!

My sweetheart is a ugly witch,
And you should see her noses twitch,—
But Goodness Me, her father's rich!
   —And I'm not Hugh nor Harry!

This is, you see, a silly song
And you can sing it all day long—
You'll find I'm either right or wrong
   —Heigho Hugh and Harry!

The moral is, I guess you keep
Yourself awake until you sleep,
And sometimes look before you leap
   —Unless you're Hugh or Harry!

A. E. HOUSMAN

As I was walking slowly
    Among the grassy hay,
Oh, there I met an old man
    Whose nerves had given way:
His heels were in an ants' nest,
    His head was in a tree,
And his arms went round and round and round
    And he squealed repeatedly.

I waited very kindly,
    And attended to his wants;
For I put his heels into the tree,
    And his head among the ants:
I tied his hands with a boot-lace,
    And I filled his mouth with hay,
And I said "Good-bye; fine morning:
    Many happy returns of the day!"

He could not squeal distinctly,
    And his arms would not go round;
Yet he did not leave off making
    A discontented sound.
I gazed at him a little while,
    As I walked among the trees,
And I said "When old men's nerves give way,
    How hard they are to please!"

# *From* SONGS FROM AN ISLAND IN THE MOON

WILLIAM BLAKE

VI

Lo! the Bat with leathern wing,
Winking and blinking,
Winking and blinking,
Winking and blinking,
Like Dr. Johnson.

*Quid.*   "O ho!" said Dr. Johnson
To Scipio Africanus,

.   .   .   .   .   .

.   .   .   .   .   .

*Suction.*   "A ha!" to Dr. Johnson
Said Scipio Africanus,

.   .   .   .   .   .

.   .   .   .   .   .

And the Cellar goes down with a step. (*Grand Chorus.*)

VII

Song of boy match-sellers

*1st Vo.*   Want Matches?
*2nd Vo.*   Yes! Yes! Yes!
*1st Vo.*   Want Matches?
*2nd Vo.*   No!

*1st Vo.*   Want Matches?
*2nd Vo.*   Yes! Yes! Yes!
*1st Vo.*   Want Matches?
*2nd Vo.*   No!

There's Doctor Clash,
And Signor Falalasole,
O they sweep in the cash
Into their purse hole!
Fa me la sol, La me fa sol!

Great A, little A,
Bouncing B!
Play away, play away,
You're out of the key!
Fa me la sol, La me fa sol!

Musicians should have
A pair of very good ears,
And long fingers and thumbs,
And not like clumsy bears.
Fa me la sol, La me fa sol!

Gentlemen! Gentlemen!
Rap! Rap! Rap!
Fiddle! Fiddle! Fiddle!
Clap! Clap! Clap!
Fa me la sol, La me fa sol!

# SILLY SONG

FEDERICO GARCÍA LORCA

*Translated by Harriet de Onis*

Mama,
I wish I were silver.

Son,
You'd be very cold.

Mama,
I wish I were water.

Son,
You'd be very cold.

Mama,
Embroider me on your pillow.

That, yes!
Right away!

# CANCION TONTA

FEDERICO GARCÍA LORCA

Mamá.
Yo quiero ser de plata.

Hijo,
tendrás mucho frío.

Mamá.
Yo quiero ser de agua.

Hijo,
tendrás mucho frío.

Mamá.
Bórdame en tu almohada.

¡Eso sí!
¡Ahora mismo!

# TO THE TERRESTRIAL GLOBE

## BY A MISERABLE WRETCH

W. S. GILBERT

Roll on, thou ball, roll on!
Through pathless realms of Space
    Roll on!
What though I'm in a sorry case?
What though I cannot meet my bills?
What though I suffer toothache's ills?
What though I swallow countless pills?
  Never *you* mind!
    Roll on!

Roll on, thou ball, roll on!
Through seas of inky air
    Roll on!
It's true I have no shirts to wear;
It's true my butcher's bill is due;
It's true my prospects all look blue—
But don't let that unsettle you:
  Never *you* mind!
    Roll on!

[*It rolls on.*

# THE SERPENT

THEODORE ROETHKE

There was a Serpent who had to sing.
There was. There was.
He simply gave up Serpenting.
Because. Because.

He didn't like his Kind of Life;
He couldn't find a proper Wife;
He was a Serpent with a soul;
He got no Pleasure down his Hole.
And so, of course, he had to Sing,
And Sing he did, like Anything!
The Birds, they were, they were Astounded;
And various Measures Propounded
To stop the Serpent's Awful Racket:
They bought a Drum. He wouldn't Whack it.
They sent,—you always send,—to Cuba
And got a Most Commodious Tuba;
They got a Horn, they got a Flute,
But Nothing would suit.
He said, "Look, Birds, all this is futile:
I do *not* like to Bang or Tootle."
And then he cut loose with a Horrible Note
That practically split the Top of his Throat.
"You see," he said, with a Serpent's Leer,
"I'm Serious about my Singing Career!"
And the Woods Resounded with many a Shriek
As the Birds flew off to the End of Next Week.

# DINKY

THEODORE ROETHKE

O what's the weather in a Beard?
It's windy there, and rather weird,
And when you think the sky has cleared
  —Why, there is Dirty Dinky.

Suppose you walk out in a Storm,
Without nothing on to keep you warm,
And then step barefoot on a Worm
  —Of course, it's Dirty Dinky.

As I was crossing a hot hot Plain,
I saw a sight that caused me pain,
You asked me before, I'll tell you again:
  —It *looked* like Dirty Dinky.

Last night you lay a-sleeping? No!
The room was thirty-five below;
The sheets and blankets turned to snow.
  —He'd got in: Dirty Dinky.

You'd better watch the things you do.
You'd better watch the things you do.
You're part of him; he's part of you
  —*You* may be Dirty Dinky.

Away with bloodshed, I love not such,
But Jane Eliza snores too much.

I bought a serpent that bites and stings
For three-and-sixpence or four shillings.

When Jane Eliza began to snore
I put it under her bedroom door.

The serpent had neither bit nor stung,
It had only just put out its tongue,

When Jane Eliza fell out of bed
And bumped upon it and killed it dead.

It showed off none of its pretty tricks
That cost four shillings or three-and-six;

It had no time to sting or bite
Nor even to utter the words "Good night".

So three-and-sixpence at least is gone,
And Jane Eliza, she still snores on.

# ECLOGUE

## COMPOSED AT CANNES,
## DECEMBER 9th, 1867

EDWARD LEAR

(*Interlocutors—Mr. Lear and Mr. and Mrs. Symonds.*)

Edwardus.—What makes you look so black, so glum, so cross?
       Is it neuralgia, headache, or remorse?

Johannes.—What makes you look as cross, or even more so?
       Less like a man than is a broken Torso?

E.—What if my life is odious, should I grin?
       If you are savage, need I care a pin?

J.—And if I suffer, am I then an owl?
       May I not frown and grind my teeth and growl?

E.—Of course you may; but may not I growl too?
       May I not frown and grind my teeth like you?

J.—See Catherine comes! To her, to her,
       Let each his several miseries refer;
       She shall decide whose woes are least or worst,
       And which, as growler, shall rank last or first.

Catherine.—Proceed to growl, in silence I'll attend,
       And hear your foolish growlings to the end;
       And when they're done, I shall correctly judge
       Which of your griefs are real or only fudge.
       Begin, let each his mournful voice prepare,
       (And pray, however angry, do not swear!)

J.—We came abroad for warmth, and find sharp cold!
　　Cannes is an imposition, and we're sold.

E.—Why did I leave my native land, to find
　　Sharp hailstones, snow, and most disgusting wind?

J.—What boots it that we orange trees or lemons see,
　　If we must suffer from *such* vile inclemency?

E.—Why did I take the lodgings I have got,
　　Where all I don't want is:—all I want not?

J.—Last week I called aloud, O! O! O! O!
　　The ground is wholly overspread with snow!
　　Is that at any rate a theme for mirth
　　Which makes a sugar-cake of all the earth?

E.—Why must I sneeze and snuffle, groan and cough,
　　If my hat's on my head, or if it's off?
　　Why must I sink all poetry in this prose,
　　The everlasting blowing of my nose?

J.—When I walk out the mud my footsteps clogs,
　　Besides, I suffer from attacks of dogs.

E.—Me a vast awful bulldog, black and brown,
　　Completely terrified when near the town;
　　As calves, perceiving butchers, trembling reel,
　　So did *my* calves the approaching monster feel.

J.—Already from two rooms we're driven away,
　　Because the beastly chimneys smoke all day:
　　Is this a trifle, say? Is this a joke?
　　That we, like hams, should be becooked in
　　　　smoke?

E.—Say, what avails it that my servant speaks
  Italian, English, Arabic, and Greek,
  Besides Albanian: if he don't speak French,
  How can he ask for salt, or shrimps, or tench?

J.—When on the foolish hearth fresh wood I place,
  It whistles, sings, and squeaks, before my face:
  And if it does unless the fire burns bright,
  And if it does, yet squeaks, how can I write?

E.—Alas! I needs must go and call on swells,
  That they may say, "Pray draw me the Estrelles."
  On one I went last week to leave a card,
  The swell was out—the servant eyed me hard:
  "This chap's a thief disguised," his face expressed:
  If I go there again, may I be blest!

J.—Why must I suffer in this wind and gloom?
  Roomattics in a vile cold attic room?

E.—Swells drive about the road with haste and fury,
  As Jehu drove about all over Jewry.
  Just now, while walking slowly, I was all but
  Run over by the Lady Emma Talbot,
  Whom not long since a lovely babe I knew,
  With eyes and cap-ribbons of perfect blue.

J.—Downstairs and upstairs, every blessed minute,
  There's each room with pianofortes in it.
  How can I write with noises such as those?
  And, being always discomposed, compose?

E.—Seven Germans through my garden lately strayed,

And all on instruments of torture played:
They blew, they screamed, they yelled: how can I
 paint
Unless my room is quiet, which it ain't?

J.—How can I study if a hundred flies
Each moment blunder into my eyes?

E.—How can I draw with green or blue or red,
If flies and beetles vex my old bald head?

J.—How can I translate German Metaphys—
—Ics, if mosquitoes round my forehead whizz?

E.—I've bought some bacon (though it's much too fat),
But round the house there prowls a hideous cat:
Once should I see my bacon in her mouth,
What care I if my rooms look north or south?

J.—Pain from a pane in one cracked window comes,
Which sings and whistles, buzzes, shrieks and
 hums;
In vain amain with pain the pane with this chord
I fain would strain to stop the beastly *dis*cord!

E.—If rain and wind and snow and such like ills
Continue here, how shall I pay my bills?
For who through cold and slush and rain will come
To see my drawings and to purchase some?
And if they don't, what destiny is mine?
How can I ever get to Palestine?

J.—The blinding sun strikes through the olive trees,
When I walk out, and always makes me sneeze.

77

E.—Next door, if all night long the moon is shining,
    There sits a dog, who wakes me up with whining.

Cath. —Forbear! You both are bores, you've growled
        enough:
    No longer will I listen to such stuff!
    All men have nuisances and bores to afflict 'um:
    Hark then, and bow to my official dictum!
    For you, Johannes, there is most excuse,
    (Some interruptions are the very deuce),
    You're younger than the other cove, who surely
    Might have some sense—besides, you're somewhat
        poorly.
    This therefore is my sentence, that you nurse
    The Baby for seven hours, and nothing worse.
    For you, Edwardus, I shall say no more
    Than that your griefs are fudge, yourself a bore:
    Return at once to cold, stewed, minced, hashed
        mutton—
    To wristbands ever guiltless of a button—
    To raging winds and sea (where don't you wish
    Your luck may ever let you catch one fish?)—

    To make large drawings nobody will buy—
    To paint oil pictures which will never dry—
    To write new books which nobody will read—
    To drink weak tea, on tough old pigs to feed—
    Till spring-time brings the birds and leaves and
        flowers,
    And time restores a world of happier hours.

"Come away, O human child!"

W. B. YEATS

# THE DEVIL'S BAG

JAMES STEPHENS

I saw the Devil walking down the lane
Behind our house.—A heavy bag
Was strapped upon his shoulders and the rain
Sizzled when it hit him.
He picked a rag
Up from the ground and put it in his sack,
And grinned, and rubbed his hands.
There was a thing
Alive inside the bag upon his back
—It must have been a soul! I saw it fling
And twist about inside, and not a hole
Or cranny for escape! Oh, it was sad!
I cried, and shouted out,—*Let out that soul!*
But he turned round, and, sure, his face went mad,
And twisted up and down, and he said "*Hell!*"
And ran away . . . Oh, mammy! I'm not well!

# PRESENTIMENT

RAINER MARIA RILKE

*Translated by M. D. Herter Norton*

I am like a flag by far spaces surrounded.
I sense the winds that are coming, I must live them
while things down below are not yet moving:
the doors are still shutting gently, and in the chimneys is silence;
the windows are not yet trembling, and the dust is still heavy.

Then already I know the storms and am stirred like the sea.
And spread myself out and fall back into myself
and fling myself off and am all alone
in the great storm.

# VORGEFÜHL

RAINER MARIA RILKE

Ich bin wie eine Fahne von Fernen umgeben.
Ich ahne die Winde, die kommen, ich muss sie leben,
während die Dinge unten sich noch nicht rühren:
die Türen schliessen noch sanft, und in den Kaminen ist Stille;
die Fenster zittern noch nict, und der Staub ist noch schwer.

Da weiss ich die Stürme schon und bin erregt wie das Meer.
Und breite mich aus und falle in mich hinein
und werfe mich ab und bin ganz allein
in dem grossen Sturm.

# FRAGMENT OF A BYLINA

ALEKSANDER PUSHKIN

*Translated by Jane Harrison and Hope Mirrlees*

In the springtime, the warm time, the soft time,
Just before the white hour of the dawning
From the forest, the forest a-dreaming,
There came forth a brown bear, a great she-bear
With her children, her little ones, bear-cubs,
To see and be seen and to gambol.

And the she-bear sat down 'neath a birchtree,
And the bear-cubs they played with each other,
With each other they rolled and they tumbled.
And—from heaven knows where—came a peasant,
In his hands was a spear for his hunting,
At his belt hung a knife for the flaying,
And a sack it hung down from his shoulders.
When the she-bear was ware of the peasant
With his spear, then she roared, did the she-bear,
And straightway she called to her children,
To those foolish ones, thoughtless young bear-cubs:
"Oh my children, my bear-cubs, my little ones,
"Stop fooling and somersaults turning,
"Stop your fondling, take shelter behind me.
"That peasant shall never get at you,
"That peasant, I'll eat out his belly."
The bear-cubs were frightened, so frightened,
They all rushed behind their bear-mother.
But the she-bear was terribly angry,
In her wrath she rose up on her hind-paws,
But that peasant knew what she was after,
With his spear he rushed straight on the she-bear,

And he struck her just over her navel,
And the she-bear fell down on the damp earth.
And the peasant ripped open her belly,
And stripped off her hide from the she-bear,
And into his sack put the bear-cubs.
And he shouldered his sack and went homewards.
"Ho my wife, here! for you a fine present,
"Here's a bear-coat that's worth fifty roubles,
"And here too's another fine present,
"Here are bear-cubs and each worth five roubles."

It was not the bells that were ringing
Thro' the town, 'twas the news they were bringing
Thro' the wood to the bear, to the black one
That a peasant had slaughtered his she-bear,
And into the sack put the bear-cubs.
The bear hung his head in dejection
And lifted his voice in lamenting
For his lady, his love, his brown she-bear.
"Oh my love, oh my life, my brown she-bear,
"Oh why hast thou left me, bereft me,
"A widower disconsolate left me?
"Nevermore shall we two play together,
"Nevermore shalt thou bear me sweet bear-cubs,
"Nevermore in my arms shall I toss them,
"And rock them, and sing them to slumber."

Then the wild beasts all gathered together,
To the Bear, to their Lord and their Master.
And together the big beasts came running,
And together came running the small beasts,
And the wolf, he came up, a wolf franklin,
And his teeth they were sharp for the biting,
And his eyes they were green for the grudging.

And the beaver came up, the guild-merchant,
And fat was the tail of the beaver.
And a weasel came up, of position,
And a squirrel, too, came, a young princess.
And a vixen came up, a clerk's missis—
A clerk to the Royal Exchequer.
And there came, too, an ermine, a mummer,
And a hare came up running, a hare-serf,
A grey hare that was piteous to look at.
And the marmot came up, a barn-stormer—
Behind in the barn lived the marmot—
And a publican hedgehog came running.
And that hedgehog was always hedgehogging,
And always his bristles were bristling.

*　　　*　　　*


# СКАЗКА О МЕДВЕДИХЕ

А. С. ПУШКИН

Как весенней теплою порою
Из-под утренней белой зорюшки,
Что из лесу, из лесу из дремучего
Выходила бурая медведиха
Со милыми детушками медвежатами
Погулять, посмотреть, себя показать.
Села медведиха под белой березою;
Стали медвежата промеж собой играть
По муравушке валятися,
Боротися, кувыркатися.
Отколь ни возьмись мужик идет,
Он в руках несет рогатину,
А нож-то у него за поясом,
А мешок-то у него за плечьями.

Как завидела медведиха
Мужика со рогатиной,
Заревела медведиха,
Стала кликать малых детушек,
Своих глупых медвежатушек.
Ах вы детушки, медвежатушки
Перестаньте играть, валятися
Боротися, кувыркатися.
Уж как знать на нас мужик идет,
Становитесь, хоронитесь за меня,
Уж как я вас мужику не выдам,
И сама мужику . . . выем.

Медвежатушки испугалися,
За медведиху бросалися,
А медведиха осержалася,
На дыбы подымалася.
А мужик-от он догадлив был,
Он пускался на медведиху,
Он сажал в нее рогатину,
Что повыше пупа, пониже печени.
Грянулась медведиха о сыру землю;
А мужик-то ей брюхо порол,
Брюхо порол, да шкуру снимал,
Малых медвежатушек в мешок поклал,
А поклавши-то домой пошел.

« Вот тебе, жена, подарочек,
Что медвежья шуба в пятьдесят рублев,
А что вот тебе другой подарочек,
Трои медвежата по пять рублев. »

Не звоны пошли по городу,
Пошли вести по всему по лесу,
Дошли вести до медведя чернобурого,
Что убил мужик его медведиху,
Распорол ей брюхо белое,

Брюхо распорол да шкуру сымал,
Медвежатушек в мешок поклал.
В ту пору медведь запечалился,
Голову повесил, голосом завыл
Про свою ли сударушку,
Чернобурую медведиху.
—Ах ты свет моя медведиха,
На кого меня покинула,
Вдовца печального,
Вдовца горемычного?
Уж как мне с тобой, моей боярыней,
Веселой игры не игрывати,
Милых детушек не родити,
Медвежатушек не качати,
Не качати, не баюкати.—
В ту пору звери собиралися
Ко тому ли медведю, к большому боярину.
Приходили звери большие,
Прибегали тут зверишки меньшие,
Прибегал тут волк дворянин,
У него-то зубы закусливые,
У него-то глаза завистливые.
Приходил тут бобр, торговый гость,
У него-то бобра жирный хвост.
Приходила ласточка дворяночка,
Приходила белочка княгинечка,
Приходила лисица подъячиха,
Подъячиха казначеиха,
Приходил скоморох горностаюшка,
Приходул байбак тут игумен
Жувет он байбак позадь гумен.
Прибегал тут зайка-смерд,
Зайка беленький, зайка серенький,
Приходил целовальник еж,
Все-то еж он ежится,
Все-то он щетинится.

# THE APPLE TREE

JAMES STEPHENS

I was hiding in the crooked apple tree,
Scouting for Indians, when a man came!
I thought it was an Indian, for he
Was running like the wind—There was a flame
Of sunlight on his hand as he drew near,
And then I saw a knife gripped in his fist!

He panted like a horse!   His eyes were queer!
Wide-open!   Staring frightfully!   And, hist!
His mouth stared open like another eye!
And all his hair was matted down with sweat!

I crouched among the leaves lest he should spy
Where I was hiding—So he did not get
His awful eyes on me; but, like the wind,
He fled, as if he heard some thing behind!

# DWARVES' SONG

## From *The Hobbit*

J. R. R. TOLKIEN

Chip the glasses and crack the plates!
    Blunt the knives and bend the forks!
That's what Bilbo Baggins hates—
    Smash the bottles and burn the corks!

Cut the cloth and tread on the fat!
    Pour the milk on the pantry floor!
Leave the bones on the bedroom mat!
    Splash the wine on every door!

Dump the crocks in a boiling bowl;
    Pound them up with a thumping pole;
And when you're finished, if any are whole,
    Send them down the hall to roll!

That's what Bilbo Baggins hates!
So, carefully! carefully with the plates!

# THE HOST OF THE AIR

W. B. YEATS

O'Driscoll drove with a song
The wild duck and the drake
From the tall and the tufted reeds
Of the drear Hart Lake.

And he saw how the reeds grew dark
At the coming of night-tide,
And dreamed of the long dim hair
Of Bridget his bride.

He heard while he sang and dreamed
A piper piping away,
And never was piping so sad,
And never was piping so gay.

And he saw young men and young girls
Who danced on a level place,
And Bridget his bride among them,
With a sad and a gay face.

The dancers crowded about him
And many a sweet thing said,
And a young man brought him red wine
And a young girl white bread.

But Bridget drew him by the sleeve
Away from the merry bands,
To old men playing at cards
With a twinkling of ancient hands.

The bread and the wine had a doom,
For these were the host of the air;
He sat and played in a dream
Of her long dim hair.

He played with the merry old men
And thought not of evil chance,
Until one bore Bridget his bride
Away from the merry dance.

He bore her away in his arms,
The handsomest young man there,
And his neck and his breast and his arms
Were drowned in her long dim hair.

O'Driscoll scattered the cards
And out of his dreams awoke:
Old men and young men and young girls
Were gone like a drifting smoke;

But he heard high up in the air
A piper piping away,
And never was piping so sad,
And never was piping so gay.

# THE ADVENTURES OF TOM BOMBADIL

J. R. R. TOLKIEN

Old Tom Bombadil was a merry fellow;
bright blue his jacket was and his boots were yellow,
green were his girdle and his breeches all of leather;
he wore in his tall hat a swan-wing feather.
He lived up under Hill, where the Withywindle
ran from a grassy well down into the dingle.

Old Tom in summertime walked about the meadows
gathering the buttercups, running after shadows,
tickling the bumblebees that buzzed among the flowers,
sitting by the waterside for hours upon hours.

There his beard dangled long down into the water:
up came Goldberry, the River-woman's daughter;
pulled Tom's hanging hair. In he went a-wallowing
under the water-lilies, bubbling and a-swallowing.

"Hey, Tom Bombadil! Whither are you going?"
said fair Goldberry. "Bubbles you are blowing,
frightening the finny fish and the brown water-rat,
startling the dabchicks, and drowning your feather-hat!"

"You bring it back again, there's a pretty maiden!"
said Tom Bombadil. "I do not care for wading.
Go down! Sleep again where the pools are shady
far below willow-roots, little water-lady!"

Back to her mother's house in the deepest hollow
swam young Goldberry. But Tom, he would not follow;

on knotted willow-roots he sat in sunny weather,
drying his yellow boots and his draggled feather.

Up woke Willow-man, began upon his singing,
sang Tom fast asleep under branches swinging;
in a crack caught him tight: snick! it closed together,
trapped Tom Bombadil, coat and hat and feather.

"Ha, Tom Bombadil! What be you a-thinking,
peeping inside my tree, watching me a-drinking
deep in my wooden house, tickling me with feather,
dripping wet down my face like a rainy weather?"

"You let me out again, Old Man Willow!
I am stiff lying here; they're no sort of pillow,
your hard crooked roots. Drink your river-water!
Go back to sleep again like the River-daughter!"

Willow-man let him loose when he heard him speaking;
locked fast his wooden house, muttering and creaking,
whispering inside the tree. Out from willow-dingle
Tom went walking on up the Withywindle.
Under the forest-eaves he sat a while a-listening:
on the boughs piping birds were chirruping and whistling.
Butterflies about his head went quivering and winking,
until grey clouds came up, as the sun was sinking.

Then Tom hurried on. Rain began to shiver,
round rings spattering in the running river;
a wind blew, shaken leaves chilly drops were dripping;
into a sheltering hole Old Tom went skipping.

Out came Badger-brock with his snowy forehead
and his dark blinking eyes. In the hill he quarried

with his wife and many sons. By the coat they caught him,
pulled him inside their earth, down their tunnels brought him.

Inside their secret house, there they sat a-mumbling:
"Ho, Tom Bombadil! Where have you come tumbling,
bursting in the front-door? Badger-folk have caught you.
You'll never find it out, the way that we have brought you!"

"Now, old Badger-brock, do you hear me talking?
You show me out at once! I must be a-walking.
Show me to your backdoor under briar-roses;
then clean grimy paws, wipe your earthy noses!
Go back to sleep again on your straw pillow,
like fair Goldberry and Old Man Willow!"

Then all the Badger-folk said: "We beg your pardon!"
They showed Tom out again to their thorny garden,
went back and hid themselves, a-shivering and a-shaking,
blocked up all their doors, earth together raking.

Rain had passed. The sky was clear, and in the summer-
      gloaming
Old Tom Bombadil laughed as he came homing,
unlocked his door again, and opened up a shutter.
In the kitchen round the lamp moths began to flutter;
Tom through the window saw waking stars come winking,
and the new slender moon early westward sinking.

Dark came under Hill. Tom, he lit a candle;
upstairs creaking went, turned the door-handle.
"Hoo, Tom Bombadil! Look what night has brought you!
I'm here behind the door. Now at last I've caught you!
You'd forgotten Barrow-wight dwelling in the old mound
up there on hill-top with the ring of stones round.

He's got loose again. Under earth he'll take you.
Poor Tom Bombadil, pale and cold he'll make you!"

"Go out! Shut the door, and never come back after!
Take away gleaming eyes, take your hollow laughter!
Go back to grassy mound, on your stony pillow
lay down your bony head, like Old Man Willow,
like young Goldberry, and Badger-folk in burrow!
Go back to buried gold and forgotten sorrow!"

Out fled Barrow-wight through the window leaping,
through the yard, over wall like a shadow sweeping,
up hill wailing went back to leaning stone-rings,
back under lonely mound, rattling his bone-rings.

Old Tom Bombadil lay upon his pillow
sweeter than Goldberry, quieter than the Willow,
snugger than the Badger-folk or the Barrow-dwellers;
slept like a humming-top, snored like a bellows.

He woke in morning-light, whistled like a starling,
sang, "Come derry-dol, merry-dol, my darling!"
He clapped on his battered hat, boots, and coat and feather;
opened the window wide to the sunny weather.

Wise old Bombadil, he was a wary fellow;
bright blue his jacket was, and his boots were yellow.
None ever caught old Tom in upland or in dingle,
walking the forest-paths, or by the Withywindle,
or out on the lily-pools in boat upon the water.
But one day Tom, he went and caught the River-daughter,
in green gown, flowing hair, sitting in the rushes,
singing old water-songs to birds upon the bushes.

He caught her, held her fast! Water-rats went scuttering
reeds hissed, herons cried, and her heart was fluttering.
Said Tom Bombadil: "Here's my pretty maiden!
You shall come home with me! The table is all laden:
yellow cream, honeycomb, white bread and butter;
roses at the window-sill and peeping round the shutter.
You shall come under Hill! Never mind your mother
in her deep weedy pool: there you'll find no lover!"

Old Tom Bombadil had a merry wedding,
crowned all with buttercups, hat and feather shedding;
his bride with forgetmenots and flag-lilies for garland
was robed all in silver-green. He sang like a starling,
hummed like a honey-bee, lilted to the fiddle,
clasping his river-maid round her slender middle.

Lamps gleamed within his house, and white was the bedding;
in the bright honey-moon Badger-folk came treading,
danced down under Hill, and Old Man Willow
tapped, tapped at window-pane, as they slept on the pillow,
on the bank in the reeds River-woman sighing
heard old Barrow-wight in his mound crying.

Old Tom Bombadil heeded not the voices,
taps, knocks, dancing feet, all the nightly noises;
slept till the sun arose, then sang like a starling:
"Hey! Come derry-dol, merry-dol, my darling!"
sitting on the door-step chopping sticks of willow,
while fair Goldberry combed her tresses yellow.

# THE TURN OF THE ROAD

JAMES STEPHENS

I was playing with my hoop along the road
Just where the bushes are, when, suddenly,
I heard a shout.—I ran away and stowed
Myself beneath a bush, and watched to see
What made the noise, and then, around the bend,
A woman came.

She was old!
She was wrinkle-faced!   She had big teeth!—The end
Of her red shawl caught on a bush and rolled
Right off her, and her hair fell down.—Her face
Was white, and awful, and her eyes looked sick,
And she was talking queer.

"*O God of Grace!*"
Said she, "*where is the child?*" and flew back quick
The way she came, and screamed, and shook her hands!
... Maybe she was a witch from foreign lands!

"... imaginary gardens with real toads ..."

MARIANNE MOORE

# MADNESS ONE MONDAY EVENING

JULIA FIELDS

Late that mad Monday evening
I made mermaids come from the sea
As the black sky sat
Upon the waves
And night came
Creeping up to me

       (I tell you I made mermaids
       Come from the sea)

The green waves lulled and rolled
As I sat by the locust tree
And the bright glare of the neon world
Sent gas-words bursting free—
Their spewed splendor fell on the billows
And gaudy it grew to me
As I sat up upon the shore
And made mermaids come from the sea.

# THE LIZARD IS CRYING...

FEDERICO GARCÍA LORCA

*Translated by Stephen Spender and J. L. Gili*

The he-lizard is crying.
The she-lizard is crying.

The he-lizard and the she-lizard
with little white aprons.

Have lost without wanting to
their wedding ring.

Ah, their little leaden wedding ring,
ah, their little ring of lead!

A large sky without people
carries the birds in its balloon.

The sun, rotund captain,
wears a satin waistcoat.

Look how old they are!
How old the lizards are!

Oh, how they cry and cry,
Oh! Oh! How they go on crying!

# EL LAGARTO ESTA LLORANDO . . .

FEDERICO GARCÍA LORCA

El lagarto está llorando.
La lagarta está llorando.

El lagarto y la lagarta
con delantalitos blancos.

Han perdido sin querer
su anillo de desposados.

¡Ay, su anillito de plomo,
ay, su anillito plomado!

Un cielo grande y sin gente
monta en su globo a los pájaros.

El sol, capitán redondo,
lleva un chaleco de raso.

¡Miradlos qué viejos son!
¡Qué viejos son los lagartos!

¡Ay, cómo lloran y lloran,
¡ay! ¡ay! cómo están llorando!

# MACAVITY: THE MYSTERY CAT

T. S. ELIOT

Macavity's a Mystery Cat: he's called the Hidden Paw—
For he's the master criminal who can defy the Law.
He's the bafflement of Scotland Yard, the Flying Squad's
　　despair:
For when they reach the scene of crime—*Macavity's not there!*

Macavity, Macavity, there's no one like Macavity,
He's broken every human law, he breaks the law of gravity.
His powers of levitation would make a fakir stare,
And when you reach the scene of crime—*Macavity's not there!*
You may seek him in the basement, you may look up in the air—
But I tell you once and once again, *Macavity's not there!*

Macavity's a ginger cat, he's very tall and thin;
You would know him if you saw him, for his eyes are sunken in.
His brow is deeply lined with thought, his head is highly domed;
His coat is rusty from neglect, his whiskers are uncombed.
He sways his head from side to side, with movements like a
　　snake;
And when you think he's half asleep, he's always wide awake.

Macavity, Macavity, there's no one like Macavity,
For he's a fiend in feline shape, a monster of depravity.
You may meet him in a by-street, you may see him in the
　　square—
But when a crime's discovered, then *Macavity's not there!*

He's outwardly respectable. (They say he cheats at cards.)
And his footprints are not found in any file of Scotland Yard's.
And when the larder's looted, or the jewel-case is rifled,

Or when the milk is missing, or another Peke's been stifled,
Or the greenhouse glass is broken, and the trellis past repair—
Ay, there's the wonder of the thing! *Macavity's not there!*

And when the Foreign Office find a Treaty's gone astray,
Or the Admiralty lose some plans and drawings by the way,
There may be a scrap of paper in the hall or on the stair—
But it's useless to investigate—*Macavity's not there!*
And when the loss has been disclosed, the Secret Service say:
"It *must* have been Macavity!"—but he's a mile away.
You'll be sure to find him resting, or a-licking of his thumbs,
Or engaged in doing complicated long division sums.

Macavity, Macavity, there's no one like Macavity,
There never was a Cat of such deceitfulness and suavity.
He always has an alibi, and one or two to spare:
At whatever time the deed took place—MACAVITY WASN'T
    THERE!
And they say that all the Cats whose wicked deeds are widely
    known
(I might mention Mungojerrie, I might mention Griddlebone)
Are nothing more than agents for the Cat who all the time
Just controls their operations: the Napoleon of Crime!

# THE TERM

WILLIAM CARLOS WILLIAMS

A rumpled sheet
of brown paper
about the length

and apparent bulk
of a man was
rolling with the

wind slowly over
and over in
the street as

a car drove down
upon it and
crushed it to

the ground. Unlike
a man it rose
again rolling

with the wind over
and over to be as
it was before.

# THE CENTAUR

MAY SWENSON

The summer that I was ten—
Can it be there was only one
summer that I was ten? It must

have been a long one then—
each day I'd go out to choose
a fresh horse from my stable

which was a willow grove
down by the old canal.
I'd go out on my two bare feet.

But when, with my brother's jack-knife,
I had cut me a long limber horse
with a good thick knob for a head,

and peeled him slick and clean
except a few leaves for the tail,
and cinched my brother's belt

around his head for a rein,
I'd straddle and canter him fast
up the grass bank to the path,

trot along in the lovely dust
that talcumed over his hoofs,
hiding my toes, and turning

his feet to swift half-moons.
The willow knob with the strap
jouncing between my thighs

was the pommel and yet the poll
of my nickering pony's head.
My head and my neck were mine,

yet they were shaped like a horse.
My hair flopped to the side
like the mane of a horse in the wind.

My forelock swung in my eyes,
my neck arched and I snorted.
I shied and skittered and reared,

stopped and raised my knees,
pawed at the ground and quivered.
My teeth bared as we wheeled

and swished through the dust again.
I was the horse and the rider,
and the leather I slapped to his rump

spanked my own behind.
Doubled, my two hoofs beat
a gallop along the bank,

the wind twanged in my mane,
my mouth squared to the bit.
And yet I sat on my steed

quiet, negligent riding,
my toes standing the stirrups,
my thighs hugging his ribs.

At a walk we drew up to the porch.
I tethered him to a paling.
Dismounting, I smoothed my skirt

and entered the dusky hall.
My feet on the clean linoleum
left ghostly toes in the hall.

*Where have you been?* said my mother.
*Been riding,* I said from the sink,
and filled me a glass of water.

*What's that in your pocket?* she said.
*Just my knife.* It weighted my pocket
and stretched my dress awry.

*Go tie back your hair,* said my mother,
and *Why is your mouth all green?*
*Rob Roy, he pulled some clover
as we crossed the field,* I told her.

# THE STONE TROLL

J. R. R. TOLKIEN

Troll sat alone on his seat of stone,
And munched and mumbled a bare old bone;
   For many a year he had gnawed it near,
     For meat was hard to come by.
       Done by! Gum by!
   In a cave in the hills he dwelt alone,
     And meat was hard to come by.

Up came Tom with his big boots on.
Said he to Troll: "Pray, what is yon?
   For it looks like the shin o' my nuncle Tim,
     As should be a-lyin' in graveyard.
       Caveyard! Paveyard!
   This many a year has Tim been gone,
     And I thought he were lyin' in graveyard".

"My lad", said Troll, "this bone I stole.
But what be bones that lie in a hole?
   Thy nuncle was dead as a lump o' lead,
     Afore I found his shinbone.
       Tinbone! Thinbone!
   He can spare a share for a poor old troll;
     For he don't need his shinbone".

Said Tom: "I don't see what the likes o' thee
Without axin' leave should go makin' free
   With the shank or the shin o' my father's kin;
     So hand the old bone over!
       Rover! Trover!
   Though dead he be, it belongs to he;
     So hand the old bone over!"

'For a couple o' pins", says Troll, and grins,
'I'll eat thee too, and gnaw thy shins.
  A bit o' fresh meat will go down sweet!
    I'll try my teeth on thee now.
        Hee now! See now!
  I'm tired o' gnawing old bones and skins;
    I've a mind to dine on thee now".


But just as he thought his dinner was caught,
He found his hands had hold of naught.
  Before he could mind, Tom slipped behind
    And gave him the boot to larn him.
        Warn him! Darn him!
  A bump o' the boot on the seat, Tom thought,
    Would be the way to larn him.


But harder than stone is the flesh and bone
Of a troll that sits in the hills alone.
  As well set your boot to the mountain's root,
    For the seat of a troll don't feel it.
        Peel it! Heal it!
  Old Troll laughed, when he heard Tom groan,
    And he knew his toes could feel it.


Tom's leg is game, since home he came,
And his bootless foot is lasting lame;
  But Troll don't care, and he's still there
    With the bone he boned from its owner.
        Doner! Boner!
  Troll's old seat is still the same,
    And the bone he boned from its owner!

# WHAT THE GRAY CAT SINGS

ARTHUR GUITERMAN

The Cat was once a weaver,
   A weaver, a weaver,
An old and withered weaver
  Who labored late and long;
And while she made the shuttle hum
And wove the weft and clipped the thrum,
Beside the loom with droning drum
  She sang the weaving song:
   "Pr-rrum, pr-rrum,
Thr-ree thr-reads in the thr-rum,
   Pr-rrum!"

The Cat's no more a weaver,
   A weaver, a weaver,
An old and wrinkled weaver,
  For though she did no wrong,
A witch hath changed the shape of her
That dwindled down and clothed in fur
Beside the hearth with droning purr
  She thrums her weaving song:
   "Pr-rrum, pr-rrum,
Thr-ree thr-reads in the thr-rum,
   Pr-rrum!"

hist     whist
little ghostthings
tip-toe
twinkle-toe

little twitchy
witches and tingling
goblins
hob-a-nob     hob-a-nob

little hoppy happy
toad in tweeds
tweeds
little itchy mousies

with scuttling
eyes     rustle and run     and
hidehidehide
whisk

whisk     look out for the old woman
with the wart on her nose
what she'll do to yer
nobody knows

for she knows the devil     ooch
the devil     ouch
the devil
ach     the great

green
dancing
devil
devil

devil
devil
       wheeEEE


# THE SONG OF THE JELLICLES

T. S. ELIOT

> *Jellicle Cats come out tonight,*
> *Jellicle Cats come one come all:*
> *The Jellicle Moon is shining bright—*
> *Jellicles come to the Jellicle Ball.*

Jellicle Cats are black and white,
Jellicle Cats are rather small;
Jellicle Cats are merry and bright,
And pleasant to hear when they caterwaul.
Jellicle Cats have cheerful faces,
Jellicle Cats have bright black eyes;
They like to practise their airs and graces
And wait for the Jellicle Moon to rise.

Jellicle Cats develop slowly,
Jellicle Cats are not too big;
Jellicle Cats are roly-poly,
They know how to dance a gavotte and a jig.
Until the Jellicle Moon appears
They make their toilette and take their repose:
Jellicles wash behind their ears,
Jellicles dry between their toes.

Jellicle Cats are white and black,
Jellicle Cats are of moderate size;
Jellicles jump like a jumping-jack,
Jellicle Cats have moonlit eyes.
They're quiet enough in the morning hours,
They're quiet enough in the afternoon,
Reserving their terpsichorean powers
To dance by the light of the Jellicle Moon.

Jellicle Cats are black and white,
Jellicle Cats (as I said) are small;
If it happens to be a stormy night
They will practise a caper or two in the hall.
If it happens the sun is shining bright
You would say they had nothing to do at all:
They are resting and saving themselves to be right
For the Jellicle Moon and the Jellicle Ball.

# THE ELEPHANT, OR THE FORCE OF HABIT

A. E. HOUSMAN

A tail behind, a trunk in front,
Complete the usual elephant.
The tail in front, the trunk behind
Is what you very seldom find.

If you for specimens should hunt
With trunks behind and tails in front,
That hunt would occupy you long;
The force of habit is so strong.

"Oh! Why was I born with a different face?"

WILLIAM BLAKE

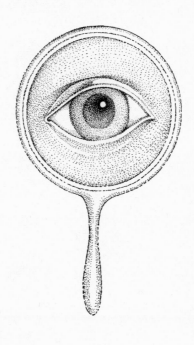

# JOHAN THE MONK

From the *Cambridge Songs*, circa 1050
*Translated by George F. Whicher*

In holy fathers' lives of old
A most amusing tale is told,
Yet not without its moral too;
I'll set it down in verse for you.

Johan the monk was far from tall,
But towered in virtue above all.
Once he addressed in fervent mood
The monk who shared his solitude.

"I wish," he said, "to shape anew
My life and live as angels do,
And what the angelic life demands
Is clothes and food not made by hands."

The elder monk replied: "My brother,
Be not more hasty than another
To undertake through vain self-will
Vows that you cannot well fulfill."

But he: "A risk is not a sin;
Risk nothing, nothing lose or win."
With that he shed his monkish dress
And naked ranged the wilderness.

Seven days of eating grass for forage
So filled his mind with thoughts of porridge
That, overcome by famine's pain,
He sought his brother monk again.

The latter lay snug in his cell;
'Twas late, the door was fastened well,
When with a voice grown weak and thin
Johan called: "Brother, let me in.

"Johan your friend, grown desperate,
Stands at this well-remembered gate;
Be not so godly as to spurn
A man whose need makes him return."

The other answered from within:
"Johan's an angel free from sin,
At heaven's gate he stands entranced,
Nor cares how men are circumstanced."

Johan was forced to camp outside,
The livelong night he must abide;
And thus he paid one penance more
Than he had ever bargained for.

When morning dawned he was let in
With scorching words of discipline,
But all rebukes he bore with patience
His thoughts were so intent on rations.

Refreshed and warmed, he thanked the Lord
And next his mate at bed and board;
Then hoed the garden, at long last,
With arms made weaker by his fast.

Thus he was taught by sharp distress
Not to indulge in flightiness.
No angel now, the monk Johan
Tries hard to be a better man.

# IN VITIS PATRUM VETERUM

In vitis patrum veterum
quiddam legi ridiculum,
exemplo tamen habile;
quod vobis dico rithmice.

Iohannes abba, parvulus
statura, non virtutibus,
ita maiori socio,
quicum erat in heremo:

"Volo," dicebat, "vivere
secure sicut angelus,
nec veste nec cibo frui,
qui laboretur manibus."

Respondit frater: "Moneo,
ne sis incepti properus,
frater, quod tibi postmodum
sit non cepisse satius."

At ille: "Qui non dimicat,
non cadit neque superat."
ait, et nudus heremum
inferiorem penetrat.

Septem dies gramineo
vix ibi durat pabulo;
octava fames imperat,
ut ad sodalem redeat.

Qui sero, clausa ianua,
tutus sedet in cellula,
cum minor voce debili
appellat: "Frater, aperi:

"Iohannes opis indigus
notis assistit foribus;
nec spernat tua pietas
quem redigit necessitas."

Respondit ille deintus:
"Iohannes, factus angelus,
miratur celi cardines;
ultra non curat homines."

Foris Iohannes excubat
malamque noctem tolerat,
et preter voluntariam
hanc agit penitentiam.

Facto mane recipitur
satisque verbis uritur;
sed intentus ad crustula
fert patienter omnia.

Refocillatus domino
grates agit et socio;
dehinc rastellum brachiis
temptat movere languidis.

Castigatus angustia
de levitate nimia,
cum angelus non potuit,
vir bonus esse didicit.

# From CONVERSATION ABOUT CHRISTMAS
### ... postmen ...

DYLAN THOMAS

With sprinkling eyes and wind-cherried noses, on spread, frozen feet they crunched up to the doors and mittened on them manfully ...

They were just ordinary postmen, fond of walking, and dogs, and Christmas, and the snow. They knocked on the doors with blue knuckles ...

And then they stood on the white welcome mat in the little, drifted porches, and clapped their hands together, and huffed and puffed, making ghosts with their breath, and jogged from foot to foot like small boys wanting to go out ...

And the cold postman, with a rose on his button-nose, tingled down the teatray-slithered run of the chilly glinting hill. He went in his ice-bound boots like a man on fishmonger's slabs. He wagged his bag like a frozen camel's hump, dizzily turned the corner on one foot, and, by God, he was gone.

# BALCONY

FEDERICO GARCÍA LORCA

*Translated by W. S. Merwin*

Lola
sings *saetas*.
The little bullfighters
circle around her
and the little barber,
from his doorway,
follows the rhythms
with his head.
Between the sweet basil
and the mint,
Lola sings
*saetas*.
That same Lola
who looked so long
at herself in the pool.

# BALCON

FEDERICO GARCÍA LORCA

La Lola
canta saetas.
Los toreritos
la rodean,
y el barberillo
desde su puerta,
sigue los ritmos
con la cabeza.
Entre la albahaca
y la hierbabuena,
la Lola canta
saetas.
La Lola aquella,
que se miraba
tanto en la alberca.

## From YOU WERE SHATTERED

GIUSEPPE UNGARETTI
*Translated by Lowry Nelson, Jr.*

You raised your arms like wings
And rendered birth to the wind,
Running in the weight of the motionless air.
No one ever saw linger
Your light and dancing feet.

## *Da* TU TI SPEZZASTI

GIUSEPPE UNGARETTI

Alzavi le braccia come ali
E ridavis nascita al vento
Correndo nel peso dell'aria immota.
Nessuno mai vide posare
Il tuo lieve piede di danza.

# DIVER

PABLO NERUDA

*Translated by Ben Belitt*

The rubber man
rose from the sea.

Seated,
he seemed
like a globular
king
of the waters,
a bulbous
and secretive
cuttlefish,
the truncated
device
of invisible algae.

From their boats, in mid-ocean,
the fishermen
sink
in their rags,
blue
with the night
of the ocean:
around them arise
the great fish of phosphor,
a voltage
of fire,
they go under:
around them, the sea urchins

tumble, piling
the silt
with the splintering spite
of their hackles.

The underseas
man
thrashes the breadth of his legs;
languidly
reels
in the horror of fish gut:
gulls
slash
the limitless air
with their hurrying scissors;
the diver
toils
through the sand
like a drunkard,
swarthy
and comatose,
locked
into his clothing, cetacean,
half-earthen,
half-ocean,
going nowhere,
inept
in the rubbery bulk
of his feet.

He goes on to his birth-throes.
The ocean
gives way
like a womb

to this innocent:
he floats sullen
and strengthless
and barbarous,
like
the
newly born.
Time after time
he takes hold of the water, the sand,
and is
born again.
Submerging
each day
to the hold
of the pitiless
current,
Pacific and
Chilean
cold,
the diver
must practice
his
birth again,
make himself
monstrous
and tentative,
displace himself
fearfully,
grow wise
in his slothful
mobility, like
an underseas
moon.
Even

his thinking
must merge
with the water:
he harvests
inimical
fruits, stalactites,
treasures,
in the pit of a solitude
drenched
with the wash
of those graveyards—
as others
would turn up a cauliflower,
he comes up
to the light—
black air in a bubble—
to Mercedes,
Clara, Rosaura.
It is painful
to walk like a man again,
to think as a man thinks, to eat
again.
All
is beginning again
for
the bulking,
ambiguous man
staggering still
in the dark
of two different abysses.

This I know—
do I not?—
as I know my existence: all

things I have seen and considered.
The way of the diver
is hazardous? The vocation
is
infinite.

## ODA AL BUZO

PABLO NERUDA

Salió el hombre de goma
de los mares.

Sentado
parecía
rey
redondo
del agua,
pulpo
secreto
y gordo,
talle
tronchado
de invisible alga.

Del oceánico bote
bajaron
pescadores
harapientos,
morados
por la noche

en el océano,
bajaron
levantando
largos peces fosfóricos
como
fuego voltaico,
los erizos cayendo
amontonaron
sobre las arenas
el rencor quebradizo
de sus púas.

El hombre
submarino
sacó sus grandes piernas,
torpemente
tambaleó entre intestinos
horribles de pescado.
Las gaviotas cortaban
el aire libre con
sus veloces tijeras,
y el buzo
como un ebrio
caminaba
en la playa,
torpe
y hosco,
enfundado
no sólo
en su vestido de cetáceo,
sino aún
medio mar
y medio tierra,
sin saber cómo

dirigir los inmensos
pies de goma.

Allí estaba naciendo.
Se desprendió
de mar
como del útero,
inocente,
y era sombrío, débil
y salvaje,
como
un
recién
nacido.
Cada vez
le tocaba
nacer
para las aguas
o la arena.
Cada día
bajando
de la proa
a las crueles
corrientes,
al frío
de Pacífico
chileno,
el buzo
tenía
que nacer,
hacerse
monstruo,
sombra
avanzar

con cautela,
aprender
a moverse
con lentitud
de luna
submarina,
tener
apenas
pensamientos
de agua,
recoger
los hostiles
frutos, estalactitas,
o tesoros
de la profunda soledad
de aquellos
mojados
cementerios,
como si recogiera
coliflores,
y cuando como un globo
de aire negro
subía
hacia
la luz, hacia
su Mercedes,
su Clara, su Rosaura,
era difícil
andar,
pensar, comer
de nuevo.
Todo
era comienzo
para
aquel hombre tan grande

todavía inconcluso,
tambaleante
entre la oscuridad
de dos abismos.

Como todas las cosas
que aprendí
en mi existencia,
viéndolas, conociendo,
aprendí que ser buzo
es un oficio
difícil? No!
Infinito.

# SCHOOLMASTER

YEVGENY YEVTUSHENKO

*Translated by Robin Milner-Gulland and Peter Levi, S. J.*

The window gives onto the white trees.
The master looks out of it at the trees,
for a long time, he looks for a long time
out through the window at the trees,
breaking his chalk slowly in one hand.
And it's only the rules of long division.
And he's forgotten the rules of long division.
Imagine not remembering long division!
A mistake on the blackboard, a mistake.
We watch him with a different attention
needing no one to hint to us about it,
there's more than difference in this attention.
The schoolmaster's wife has gone away,
we do not know where she has gone to,
we do not know why she has gone,
what we know is his wife has gone away.

His clothes are neither new nor in the fashion;
wearing the suit which he always wears
and which is neither new nor in the fashion
the master goes downstairs to the cloakroom.
He fumbles in his pocket for a ticket.
"What's the matter? Where is that ticket?
Perhaps I never picked up my ticket.
Where is the thing?" Rubbing his forehead.
"Oh, here it is. I'm getting old.
Don't argue auntie dear, I'm getting old.
You can't do much about getting old."
We hear the door below creaking behind him.

The window gives onto the white trees.
The trees there are high and wonderful,
but they are not why we are looking out.
We look in silence at the schoolmaster.
He has a bent back and clumsy walk,
he moves without defences, clumsily,
worn out I ought to have said, clumsily.
Snow falling on him softly through silence
turns him to white under the white trees.
He whitens into white like the trees.
A little longer will make him so white
we shall not see him in the whitened trees.


## ОКНО ВЫХОДИТ В БЕЛЫЕ ДЕРЕВЬЯ...

ЕВГЕНИЙ ЕВТУШЕНКО

Окно выходит в белые деревья.
Профессор долго смотрит на деревья,
Он очень долго смотрит на деревья
и очень долго мел крошит в руке.
Ведь это просто—
                        правила деленья!
А он забыл их—
                        правила деленья!
Забыл—
        подумать!—
                        правила деленья.
Ошибка!
        Да!
            Ошибка на доске!

Мы слушаем и смотрим по-другому,
да и нельзя сейчас не по-другому,
и нам подсказка в этом не нужна.
Ушла жена профессора из дома.
Не знаем мы,
                    куда ушла из дома
не знаем,
                    отчего ушла из дома
а знаем только, что ушла она.


В костюме и немодном и неновом,
как и всегда немодном и неновом,
спускается профессор в гардероб.
Он долго по карманам ищет номер:
« Ну что такое?
                    Где же этот номер?
А может быть,
                    не брал у вас я номер?
Куда он делся?—
                    Трёт руко́ю лоб.—
Ах вот он!...
            Что ж,
                    как видно, я старею.
Не спорьте, тётя Маша,
                          я старею.
И что уж тут поделаешь—
                          старею ...»
Мы слышим—
            дверь внизу скрипит за ним.
Окно выходит в белые деревья,
в большие и красивые деревья,
но мы сейчас глядим не на деревья—
мы молча на профессора глядим.

Уходит он,
                сутулый,
                        неумелый,
какой-то беззащитно неумелый,
я бы сказал—
                устало неумелый,
под снегом, мягко падающим в тишь.
Уже и сам он, как деревья, белый,
да,
    как деревья,
                совершенно белый,
ещё немного—
                и настолько белый,
что среди них его не разглядишь.

# THE OLD MEN ADMIRING THEMSELVES
## IN THE WATER

W. B. YEATS

I heard the old, old men say,
"Everything alters,
And one by one we drop away."
They had hands like claws, and their knees
Were twisted like the old thorn-trees
By the waters.
I heard the old, old men say,
"All that's beautiful drifts away
Like the waters."

# THE BALLAD OF THE
## LIGHT-EYED LITTLE GIRL

GWENDOLYN BROOKS

Sweet Sally took a cardboard box,
And in went pigeon poor.
Whom she had starved to death but not
For lack of love, be sure.

The wind it harped as twenty men.
The wind it harped like hate.
It whipped our light-eyed little girl,
It made her wince and wait.

It screeched a hundred elegies
As it punished her light eyes
(Though only kindness covered these)
And it made her eyebrows rise.

"Now bury your bird," the wind it bawled,
"And bury him down and down
Who had to put his trust in one
So light-eyed and so brown.

"So light-eyed and so villainous,
Who whooped and who could hum
But could not find the time to toss
Confederate his crumb."

She has taken her passive pigeon poor,
She has buried him down and down.
He never shall sally to Sally
Nor soil any roofs of the town.

She has sprinkled nail polish on dead dandelions.
And children have gathered around
Funeral for him whose epitaph
Is "PIGEON—Under the ground."

# COAL FOR MIKE

BERTOLT BRECHT

*Translated by H. R. Hays*

I have heard how in Ohio
At the beginning of this century
A woman lived in Bidwell,
Mary McCoy, widow of a brakeman,
By the name of Mike McCoy,
Lived in poverty.

But every night from the thundering trains of the Wheeling
    Railroad
The brakemen heaved some lumps of coal
Over the picket fence into the potato patch,
Shouting briefly in harsh voices:
For Mike!

And every night
As the lumps of coal for Mike
Crashed against the rear wall of the hut
The old woman arose, crept,
Drunk with sleep, into an overcoat and heaped
The lumps of coal to one side,
The lumps of coal,
Gift of the brakemen to Mike, dead
But not forgotten.

And she arose so long before daybreak and heaped
Her gifts away from the eyes of the world so that
The men would not get into trouble
With the Wheeling Railroad.

*This poem is dedicated to the comrades*
*Of the brakeman Mike McCoy*
(*Died from a weakness of the lungs*
*On an Ohio coal train*)
*For comradeship.*

## KOHLEN FÜR MIKE

BERTOLT BRECHT

Ich habe gehört, dass in Ohio
Zu Beginn dieses Jahrhunderts
Ein Weib wohnte zu Bidwell,
Mary McCoy, Witwe eines Bremsers,
Mit Namen Mike McCoy, in Armut.

Aber jede Nacht von den donnernden Zügen der Wheeling
    Railroad
Warfen die Bremser einen Kohlenklumpen
Über die Zaunlatten in den Kartoffelgarten
Mit rauher Stimme ausrufend in Eile:
Für Mike!

Und jede Nacht, wenn
Der Kohlenklumpen für Mike
An die Rückwand der Hütte schlug
Erhob sich die Alte, kroch,
Schlaftrunken in den Rock und räumte zur Seite
Den Kohlenklumpen
Geschenk der Bremser an Mike, den Gestorbenen, aber
Nicht Vergessenen.

Sie aber erhob sich so, lange vor Morgengrauen, und räumte
Ihre Geschenke aus den Augen der Welt, damit nicht
Die Männer in Ungelegenheit kämen
Bei der Wheeling Railroad.

*Dieses Gedicht ist gewidmet den Kameraden*
*Des Bremsers Mike McCoy*
*(Gestorben wegen zu schwacher Lunge*
*Auf den Kohlenzügen Ohios)*
*Für Kameradschaft.*

E. E. CUMMINGS

Buffalo Bill's
defunct
          who used to
          ride a watersmooth-silver
                              stallion
and break onetwothreefourfive pigeonsjustlikethat
                                        Jesus
he was a handsome man
                    and what i want to know is
how do you like your blueeyed boy
Mister Death

# TO A POOR OLD WOMAN

WILLIAM CARLOS WILLIAMS

munching a plum on
the street a paper bag
of them in her hand

They taste good to her
They taste good
to her. They taste
good to her

You can see it by
the way she gives herself
to the one half
sucked out in her hand

Comforted
a solace of ripe plums
seeming to fill the air
They taste good to her

# ANASHUYA AND VIJAYA

W. B. YEATS

*A little Indian temple in the Golden Age. Around it a garden;*
*around that the forest. Anashuya, the young priestess, kneeling*
*within the temple.*

*Anashuya.* Send peace on all the lands and flickering corn.—
  O, may tranquillity walk by his elbow
  When wandering in the forest, if he love
  No other.—Hear, and may the indolent flocks
  Be plentiful.—And if he love another,
  May panthers end him.—Hear, and load our king
  With wisdom hour by hour.—May we two stand,
  When we are dead, beyond the setting suns,
  A little from the other shades apart,
  With mingling hair, and play upon one lute.

*Vijaya* [*entering and throwing a lily at her*]. Hail! hail, my
    Anashuya.

*Anashuya.*           No: be still.
  I, priestess of this temple, offer up
  Prayers for the land.

*Vijaya.*         I will wait here, Amrita.

*Anashuya.* By mighty Brahma's ever-rustling robe,
  Who is Amrita? Sorrow of all sorrows!
  Another fills your mind.

*Vijaya.*         My mother's name.

146

*Anashuya* [*sings, coming out of the temple*].
  *A sad, sad thought went by me slowly:*
  *Sigh, O you little stars! O sigh and shake your blue apparel!*
  *The sad, sad thought has gone from me now wholly:*
  *Sing, O you little stars! O sing and raise your rapturous carol*
  *To mighty Brahma, he who made you many as the sands,*
  *And laid you on the gates of evening with his quiet hands.*
                  [*Sits down on the steps of the temple.*]
  Vijaya, I have brought my evening rice;
  The sun has laid his chin on the grey wood,
  Weary, with all his poppies gathered round him.

*Vijaya.* The hour when Kama, full of sleepy laughter,
  Rises, and showers abroad his fragrant arrows,
  Piercing the twilight with their murmuring barbs.

*Anashuya.* See how the sacred old flamingoes come,
  Painting with shadow all the marble steps:
  Aged and wise, they seek their wonted perches
  Within the temple, devious walking, made
  To wander by their melancholy minds.
  Yon tall one eyes my supper; chase him away,
  Far, far away. I named him after you.
  He is a famous fisher; hour by hour
  He ruffles with his bill the minnowed streams.
  Ah! there he snaps my rice. I told you so.
  Now cuff him off. He's off! A kiss for you,
  Because you saved my rice. Have you no thanks?

*Vijaya* [*sings*]. *Sing you of her, O first few stars,*
  *Whom Brahma, touching with his finger, praises, for you hold*
  *The van of wandering quiet; ere you be too calm and old,*

*Sing, turning in your cars,*
*Sing, till you raise your hands and sigh, and from your carheads*
    *peer,*
*With all your whirling hair, and drop many an azure tear.*


*Anashuya.* What know the pilots of the stars of tears?


*Vijaya.* Their faces are all worn, and in their eyes
Flashes the fire of sadness, for they see
The icicles that famish all the North,
Where men lie frozen in the glimmering snow;
And in the flaming forests cower the lion
And lioness, with all their whimpering cubs;
And, ever pacing on the verge of things,
The phantom, Beauty, in a mist of tears;
While we alone have round us woven woods,
And feel the softness of each other's hand,
Amrita, while—


*Anashuya* [*going away from him*].
                    Ah me! you love another,
                            [*Bursting into tears.*]
And may some sudden dreadful ill befall her!


*Vijaya.* I loved another; now I love no other.
Among the mouldering of ancient woods
You live, and on the village border she,
With her old father the blind wood-cutter;
I saw her standing in her door but now.


*Anashuya.* Vijaya, swear to love her never more.


*Vijaya.* Ay, ay.

*Anashuya.*     Swear by the parents of the gods,
Dread oath, who dwell on sacred Himalay,
On the far Golden Peak; enormous shapes,
Who still were old when the great sea was young;
On their vast faces mystery and dreams;
Their hair along the mountains rolled and filled
From year to year by the unnumbered nests
Of aweless birds, and round their stirless feet
The joyous flocks of deer and antelope,
Who never hear the unforgiving hound.
Swear!

*Vijaya.*   By the parents of the gods, I swear.

*Anashuya [sings]. I have forgiven, O new star!*
  *Maybe you have not heard of us, you have come forth so*
      *newly,*
  *You hunter of the fields afar!*
  *Ah, you will know my loved one by his hunter's arrows truly,*
  *Shoot on him shafts of quietness, that he may ever keep*
  *A lonely laughter, and may kiss his hands to me in sleep.*

Farewell, Vijaya. Nay, no word, no word;
I, priestess of the temple, offer up
Prayers for the land.
                                        [*Vijaya goes.*]
              O Brahma, guard in sleep
The merry lambs and the complacent kine,
The flies below the leaves, and the young mice
In the tree roots, and all the sacred flocks
Of red flamingoes; and my love, Vijaya;
And may no restless fay with fidget finger
Trouble his sleeping: give him dreams of me.

149

# MRS. GILFILLAN

JAMES REEVES

When Mrs. Gilfillan
  Is troubled with troubles,
She flies to the kitchen
  And sits blowing bubbles.
When Mrs. Gilfillan
  Is worried by money,
When her feet are like lead
  And her head's feeling funny,
When there's too much to do,
  And the chimney is smoking,
And everything's awkward
  And wrong and provoking,
When the washing won't dry
  For the rain's never ending,
When cupboards need cleaning
  And stockings want mending,
When the neighbours complain
  Of the noise of the cat,
And she ought to be looking
  For this and for that,
And never a line comes
  From her married daughter—
Then off to the kitchen
  With soap and warm water
Goes Mrs. Gilfillan
  And all of her troubles;
And she puffs them away
  In a great cloud of bubbles.
In joyful abandon
  She puffs them and blows them,

And all round about her
  In rapture she throws them;
When round, clear and shiny
  They hang in the air,
Away like a shadow
  Goes worry and care.


## THE CRAZY WOMAN

GWENDOLYN BROOKS

I shall not sing a May song.
A May song should be gay.
I'll wait until November
And sing a song of gray.

I'll wait until November.
That is the time for me.
I'll go out in the frosty dark
And sing most terribly.

And all the little people
Will stare at me and say,
"That is the Crazy Woman
Who would not sing in May."

# HERIGER, BISHOP OF MAINZ

MANUSCRIPT OF THE ELEVENTH CENTURY
*Translated by Helen Waddell*

Heriger,
Bishop of
Mainz, saw a
Prophet who
Said he had
Been carried
Off down to
Hell.

He among
Other and
Divers things
Mentioned that
Hell is sur-
rounded by
Very thick
Woods.

Then the good
Bishop made
Smilingly
Answer: "I
Think I shall
Send to that
Pasture my
Swineherd and
Bid him take
With him my
Very lean
Pigs."

The liar said:
"I was to
Heaven trans-
lated and
Saw Christ there
Sitting and
Joyfully
Eating.

"John called the
Baptist was
Cupbearer,
Handing round
Goblets of
Excellent
Wine to the
Saints."

.    .    .

The Bishop
Said, "Wisely
Did Christ choose
The Baptist
To be his
Cupbearer,
Because he
Is known not
To drink any
Wine.

"But you are
A liar to
Say that St
Peter is

Head of the
Cooks, when he
Keeps Heaven's
Gate.

"But tell me,
What honour
Did God set
Upon you?
Where did you
Sit? And on
What did you
Sup?"

He answered:
"I sat in
A corner
And munched at
A piece of a
Lung that I
Stole from the
Cooks."

Heriger
Had him trussed
Up to a
Pillar and
Beaten with
Broom-sticks, the
While he ad-
dressed him with
Words that were
Harsh.

"If Christ to
His Table
Hereafter
Invites you,
Do not be
In future
So dirty a
Thief."


# HERIGER

Heriger, urbis
Maguntiensis
antistes, quendam
vidit prophetam
qui ad infernum
se dixit raptum.

Inde cum multas
referret causas,
subiunxit totum
esse infernum
accinctum densis
undique silvis.

Heriger illi
ridens respondit;
"meum subulcum
illuc ad pastum
volo cum macris
mittere porcis."

Vir ait falsus:
"fui translatus
in templum celi
Christumque vidi
letum sedentem
et comedentem.

Ioannes baptista
erat pincerna
atque preclari
pocula vini
porrexit cunctis
vocatis sanctis."

.    .    .

Heriger ait:
"prudenter egit
Christus Iohannem
ponens pincernam,
quoniam vinum
non bibit unquam.

Mendax probaris
cum Petrum dicis
illic magistrum
esse cocorum.
est quia summi
ianitor celi.

Honore quali
te deus celi
habuit ibi?
ubi sedisti?
volo ut narres
quid manducasses."

Respondit homo:
"angulo uno
partem pulmonis
furabar cocis:
hoc manducavi
atque recessi."

Heriger illum
iussit ad palum
loris ligari
scopisque cedi,
sermone duro
hunc arguendo:

"Si te ad suum
invitet pastum
Christus, ut secum
capias cibum
cave ne furtum
facias (spurcum)."

# THE ABBOT ADAM OF ANGERS

NINTH-CENTURY MS. OF VERONA

*Translated by Helen Waddell*

| | |
|---|---|
| Once there was an | Abbot of Angers. |
| And the name of | the first man did he bear. |
| And they say he | had a mighty thirst |
| Even beyond the | townsmen of Angers. |

*Ho and ho and ho and ho!*
*Glory be to Bacchus!*

| | |
|---|---|
| He would have his | wine all times and seasons |
| Never did a | day or night go by, |
| But it found him | wine-soaked and wavering |
| Even as a tree | that the high winds sway. |

*Ho and ho and ho and ho!*
*Glory be to Bacchus!*

| | |
|---|---|
| As to body | was he incorruptible. |
| Like a wine that's | spiced with bitter aloes |
| And as hides are | dressed and tanned with myrrh |
| So was his skin | deep-tanned with wine. |

*Ho and ho and ho and ho!*
*Glory be to Bacchus!*

| | |
|---|---|
| Nor did he like | elegantly drinking |
| From a wine cup | filled from the barrel. |
| Naught would do him | but mighty pots and pannikins |
| Pots and pans still | greater than their species. |

*Ho and ho and ho and ho!*
*Glory be to Bacchus!*

Should it hap that  the town of Angers lost him,
Never would it    see his like again.
Never see his     like for steady drinking.
Mark him well, ye townsmen of Angers.
*Ho and ho and ho and ho!*
*Glory be to Bacchus!*


## ANDECAVIS ABBAS


Andecavis      abas esse dicitur
ille nomen     primi tenet hominum;
hunc fatentur  vinum vellet bibere
super omnes    Andechavis homines.
*Eia eia eia laudes*
*Eia laudes dicamus Libero.*


Iste malet     vinum omne tempore
quem nec dies  nox nec ulla preterit
quod non vino  saturatus titubet,
velut arbor    agitata flatibus.
*Eia eia eia laudes*
*Eia laudes dicamus Libero.*


Iste gerit     corpus imputribile
vinum totum    conditum ut alove
et ut mire     corium conficitur
cutis eius     nunc cum vino tingitur.

*Eia eia eia laudes*
*Eia laudes dicamus Libero.*

| | |
|---|---|
| Iste cupa | non curat de calicem |
| vinum bonum | bibere suaviter, |
| sed patellis | atque magnis cacabis |
| et in eis | ultra modum grandibus. |

*Eia eia eia laudes*
*Eia laudes dicamus Libero.*

| | |
|---|---|
| Hunc perperdit | Andechavis civitas |
| nullum talem | ultra sibi sociat, |
| qui sic semper | vinum possit sorbere; |
| cuius facta, | cives, vobis pingite! |

*Eia eia eia laudes*
*Eia laudes dicamus Libero.*

''I learn by going where I have to go.''

THEODORE ROETHKE

# THE ARMFUL

ROBERT FROST

For every parcel I stoop down to seize,
I lose some other off my arms and knees,
And the whole pile is slipping, bottles, buns,
Extremes too hard to comprehend at once,
Yet nothing I should care to leave behind.
With all I have to hold with, hand and mind
And heart, if need be, I will do my best
To keep their building balanced at my breast.
I crouch down to prevent them as they fall;
Then sit down in the middle of them all.
I had to drop the armful in the road
And try to stack them in a better load.

YAMABE NO AKAHITO

*Translated by Kenneth Rexroth*

I wish I were close
To you as the wet skirt of
A salt girl to her body.
I think of you always.

須磨の海人の鹽燒衣の馴水なばか。
一日も君を忘れて念はむ。
赤人

# THE PREACHER:
## RUMINATES BEHIND THE SERMON

GWENDOLYN BROOKS

I think it must be lonely to be God.
Nobody loves a master. No. Despite
The bright hosannas, bright dear-Lords, and bright
Determined reverence of Sunday eyes.

Picture Jehovah striding through the hall
Of His importance, creatures running out
From servant-corners to acclaim, to shout
Appreciation of His merit's glare.

But who walks with Him?—dares to take His arm,
To slap Him on the shoulder, tweak His ear,
Buy Him a Coca-Cola or a beer,
Pooh-pooh His politics, call Him a fool?

Perhaps—who knows?—He tires of looking down.
Those eyes are never lifted. Never straight.
Perhaps sometimes He tires of being great
In solitude. Without a hand to hold.

# FERGUS AND THE DRUID

W. B. YEATS

*Fergus.* This whole day have I followed in the rocks,
  And you have changed and flowed from shape to shape,
  First as a raven on whose ancient wings
  Scarcely a feather lingered, then you seemed
  A weasel moving on from stone to stone,
  And now at last you wear a human shape,
  A thin grey man half lost in gathering night.

*Druid.* What would you, king of the proud Red Branch kings?

*Fergus.* This would I say, most wise of living souls:
  Young subtle Conchubar sat close by me
  When I gave judgment, and his words were wise,
  And what to me was burden without end,
  To him seemed easy, so I laid the crown
  Upon his head to cast away my sorrow.

*Druid.* What would you, king of the proud Red Branch kings?

*Fergus.* A king and proud! and that is my despair.
  I feast amid my people on the hill,
  And pace the woods, and drive my chariot-wheels
  In the white border of the murmuring sea;
  And still I feel the crown upon my head.

*Druid.* What would you, Fergus?

*Fergus.*                         Be no more a king
  But learn the dreaming wisdom that is yours.

*Druid.* Look on my thin grey hair and hollow cheeks
   And on these hands that may not lift the sword,
   This body trembling like a wind-blown reed.
   No woman's loved me, no man sought my help.

*Fergus.* A king is but a foolish labourer
   Who wastes his blood to be another's dream.

*Druid.* Take, if you must, this little bag of dreams;
   Unloose the cord, and they will wrap you round.

*Fergus.* I see my life go drifting like a river
   From change to change; I have been many things—
   A green drop in the surge, a gleam of light
   Upon a sword, a fir-tree on a hill,
   An old slave grinding at a heavy quern,
   A king sitting upon a chair of gold—
   And all these things were wonderful and great;
   But now I have grown nothing, knowing all.
   Ah! Druid, Druid, how great webs of sorrow
   Lay hidden in the small slate-coloured thing!

# NIGHT PRACTICE

MAY SWENSON

I
will
remember
with my breath
to make a mountain,
with my sucked-in breath
a valley, with my pushed-out
breath a mountain. I will make
a valley wider than the whisper, I
will make a higher mountain than the cry;
will with my will breathe a mountain, I will
with my will breathe a valley. I will push out
a mountain, suck in a valley, deeper than the shout
YOU MUST DIE, harder, heavier, sharper, a mountain than
the truth YOU MUST DIE. I will remember. My breath will
make a mountain. My will will remember to will. I, suck-
ing, pushing, I will breathe a valley, I will breathe a mountain.

# KING DAVID

WALTER DE LA MARE

King David was a sorrowful man:
　　No cause for sorrow had he:
And he called for the music of a hundred harps,
　　To solace his melancholy.

They played till they all fell silent:
　　Played—and play sweet did they;
But the sorrow that haunted the heart of King David
　　They could not charm away.

He rose; and in his garden
　　Walked by the moon alone,
A nightingale hidden in a cypress-tree
　　Jargoned on and on.

King David lifted his sad eyes
　　Into the dark-boughed tree—
"Tell me, thou little bird that singest,
　　Who taught my grief to thee?"

But the bird in no wise heeded;
　　And the king in the cool of the moon
Harkened to the nightingale's sorrowfulness,
　　Till all his own was gone.

# THE BOY

RAINER MARIA RILKE
*Translated by M. D. Herter Norton*

I want to become like one of those
who through the night go driving with wild horses,
with torches that like loosened hair
blow in the great wind of their chasing.
Forward I want to stand as in a skiff,
large and like a flag unfurled.
Dark, but with a helm of gold that glints
uneasily. And in a row behind me
ten men out of the selfsame darkness
with helmets that are as unstaid as mine,
now clear as glass, now dark and old and blind.
And one beside me stands and blasts us space
upon his trumpet that flashes and that screams,
and blasts us a black solitude
through which we tear like a rapid dream:
the houses fall behind us to their knees,
the streets bend slantingly to meet us,
the squares give way: we take hold of them,
with our horses rushing like a rain.

# DER KNABE

RAINER MARIA RILKE

Ich möchte einer werden so wie die,
die durch die Nacht mit wilden Pferden fahren,
mit Fackeln, die gleich aufgegangenen Haaren
in ihres Jagens grossem Winde wehn.
Vorn möcht ich stehen wie in einem Kahne,
gross und wie eine Fahne aufgerollt.
Dunkel, aber mit einem Helm von Gold,
der unruhig glänzt. Und hinter mir gereiht
zehn Männer aus derselben Dunkelheit
mit Helmen, die wie meiner unstet sind,
bald klar wie Glas, bald dunkel, alt und blind.
Und einer steht bei mir und bläst uns Raum
mit der Trompete, welche blitzt und schreit,
und bläst uns eine schwarze Einsamkeit,
durch die wir rasen wie ein rascher Traum:
die Häuser fallen hinter uns ins Knie,
die Gassen biegen sich uns schief entgegen,
die Plätze weichen aus: wir fassen sie,
und unsere Rosse rauschen wie ein Regen.

# THE DUEL

EMILY DICKINSON

I took my power in my hand
And went against the world;
'Twas not so much as David had,
But I was twice as bold.

I aimed my pebble, but myself
Was all the one that fell.
Was it Goliath was too large,
Or only I too small?

# GET UP, BLUES

JAMES A. EMANUEL

Blues
Never climb a hill
Or sit on a roof
In starlight.

Blues
Just bend low
And moan in the street
And shake a borrowed cup.

Blues
Just sit around
Sipping.
Hatching yesterdays.

Get up, Blues.
Fly.
Learn what it means
To be up high.

# THE CRADLE TRAP

LOUIS SIMPSON

A bell and a rattle,
a smell of roses,
a leather Bible,
and angry voices . . .

They say, I love you.
They shout, You must!
The light is telling
terrible stories.

But night at the window
whispers, Never mind.
Be true, be true
to your own strange kind.

—I am like a slip of comet,
Scarce worth discovery, in some corner seen
Bridging the slender difference of two stars,
Come out of space, or suddenly engender'd
By heady elements, for no man knows;
But when she sights the sun she grows and sizes
And spins her skirts out, while her central star
Shakes its cocooning mists; and so she comes
To fields or light; millions of travelling rays
Pierce her; she hangs upon the flame-cased sun,
And sucks the light as full as Gideon's fleece:
But then her tether calls her; she falls off,
And as she dwindles shreds her smock of gold
Between the sistering planets, till she comes
To single Saturn, last and solitary;
And then she goes out into the cavernous dark.
So I go out: my little sweet is done:
I have drawn heat from this contagious sun:
To not ungentle death now forth I run.

# MIRACLES

WALT WHITMAN

Why, who makes much of a miracle?
As to me I know of nothing else but miracles,
Whether I walk the streets of Manhattan,
Or dart my sight over the roofs of houses toward the sky,
Or wade with naked feet along the beach just in the edge of the
    water,
Or stand under trees in the woods,
Or talk by day with any one I love, or sleep in the bed at night
    with any one I love,
Or sit at table at dinner with the rest,
Or look at strangers opposite me riding in the car,
Or watch honey-bees busy around the hive of a summer
    forenoon,
Or animals feeding in the fields,
Or birds, or the wonderfulness of insects in the air,
Or the wonderfulness of the sundown, or of stars shining so
    quiet and bright,
Or the exquisite delicate thin curve of the new moon in spring;
These with the rest, one and all, are to me miracles,
The whole referring, yet each distinct and in its place.

To me every hour of the light and dark is a miracle,
Every cubic inch of space is a miracle,
Every square yard of the surface of the earth is spread with the
    same,
Every foot of the interior swarms with the same.

To me the sea is a continual miracle,
The fishes that swim—the rocks—the motion of the waves—
    the ships with men in them,
What stranger miracles are there?

# THE MASK OF EVIL

BERTOLT BRECHT

*Translated by H. R. Hays*

On my wall hangs a Japanese carving,
The mask of an evil demon, decorated with gold lacquer.
Sympathetically I observe
The swollen veins of the forehead, indicating
What a strain it is to be evil.

# DIE MASKE DES BÖSEN

BERTOLT BRECHT

An meiner Wand hängt ein japanisches Holzwerk,
Maske eines bösen Dämons, bemalt mit Goldlack.
Mitfühlend sehe ich
Die geschwollenen Stirnadern, andeutend
Wie anstrengend es ist, böse zu sein.

# TO MISS RÁPIDA

JUAN RAMÓN JIMÉNEZ
*Translated by H. R. Hays*

If you hurry so,
Time will fly ahead of you like a
Fleeing butterfly.

If you go slowly,
Time will walk behind you
Like a submissive ox.


# A MISS RÁPIDA

JUAN RAMÓN JIMÉNEZ

Si vas de prisa,
el tiempo volará ante ti, como una
mariposilla esquiva.

 Si vas despacio,
el tiempo irá detrás de ti,
como un buey manso.

# THE NEGRO SPEAKS OF RIVERS
## (To W. E. B. DuBois)

LANGSTON HUGHES

I've known rivers:
I've known rivers ancient as the world and older than the
flow of human blood in human veins.

My soul has grown deep like the rivers.

I bathed in the Euphrates when dawns were young.
I built my hut near the Congo and it lulled me to sleep.
I looked upon the Nile and raised the pyramids above it.
I heard the singing of the Mississippi when Abe Lincoln
went down to New Orleans, and I've seen its muddy
bosom turn all golden in the sunset.

I've known rivers:
Ancient, dusky rivers.

My soul has grown deep like the rivers.

# *From* SEXT

W. H. AUDEN

1.

You need not see what someone is doing
to know if it is his vocation,

you have only to watch his eyes:
a cook mixing a sauce, a surgeon

making a primary incision,
a clerk completing a bill of lading,

wear the same rapt expression,
forgetting themselves in a function.

How beautiful it is,
that eye-on-the-object look.

       *       *       *

2.

You need not hear what orders he is giving
to know if someone has authority,

you have only to watch his mouth:
when a besieging general sees

a city wall breached by his troops,
when a bacteriologist

realizes in a flash what was wrong
with his hypothesis, when,

from a glance at the jury, the prosecutor
knows the defendant will hang,

their lips and the lines around them
relax, assuming an expression,

not of simple pleasure at getting
their own sweet way but of satisfaction

of being right . . .


# THE RIVER-MERCHANT'S WIFE: A LETTER

LI PO (RIHAKU)
*Translated by Ezra Pound*

While my hair was still cut straight across my forehead
I played about the front gate, pulling flowers.
You came by on bamboo stilts, playing horse,
You walked about my seat, playing with blue plums.
And we went on living in the village of Chokan:
Two small people, without dislike or suspicion.

At fourteen I married My Lord you.
I never laughed, being bashful.
Lowering my head, I looked at the wall.
Called to, a thousand times, I never looked back.

At fifteen I stopped scowling,
I desired my dust to be mingled with yours
Forever and forever and forever.
Why should I climb the look out?

At sixteen you departed,
You went into far Ku-to-yen, by the river of swirling eddies,
And you have been gone five months.
The monkeys make sorrowful music overhead.

You dragged your feet when you went out.
By the gate now, the moss is grown, the different mosses,
Too deep to clear them away!
The leaves fall early this autumn, in wind.
The paired butterflies are already yellow with August
Over the grass in the West garden;
They hurt me. I grow older.
If you are coming down through the narrows of the river Kiang,
Please let me know beforehand,
And I will come out to meet you
                    As far as Cho-fu-Sa.

## 長干行

妾髮初覆額。折花門前劇。郎騎竹馬來。遶牀弄青梅。同居長干里。兩小無嫌猜。十四爲君婦。羞顏未嘗開。低頭向暗壁。千喚不一廻。十五始展眉。願同塵與灰。常存抱柱信。豈上望夫臺。十六君遠行。瞿塘灩澦堆。五月不可觸。猿聲天上哀。門前遲行跡。一一生綠苔。苔深不能掃。落葉秋風早。八月蝴蝶黃。雙飛西園草。感此傷妾心。坐愁紅顏老。早晚下三巴。預將書報家。相迎不道遠。直至長風沙。

李白

"What was the name of that cat?"

"Cómo se llamaba aquel gato?"

PABLO NERUDA

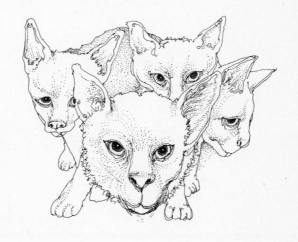

## *From* SONG OF MYSELF

WALT WHITMAN

I think I could turn and live with animals, they are so placid
    and self-contain'd,
I stand and look at them long and long.

They do not sweat and whine about their condition,
They do not lie awake in the dark and weep for their sins,
They do not make me sick discussing their duty to God,
Not one is dissatisfied, not one is demented with the mania of
    owning things,
Not one kneels to another, nor to his kind that lived thousands
    of years ago,
Not one is respectable or unhappy over the whole earth . . .

# THE PRAYER OF THE OX

CARMEN BERNOS DE GASZTOLD

*Translated by Rumer Godden*

Dear God, give me time.
Men are always so driven!
Make them understand that I can never hurry.
Give me time to eat.
Give me time to plod.
Give me time to sleep.
Give me time to think.

Amen

# PRIÈRE DU BŒUF

CARMEN BERNOS DE GASZTOLD

Mon Dieu, donnez-moi du temps.
Les hommes sont toujours pressés!
Faites-leur comprendre que je ne peux
pas aller vite.
Donnez-moi le temps de manger.
Donnez-moi le temps de marcher.
Donnez-moi le temps de dormir.
Donnez-moi le temps de penser.

Ainsi soit-il!

# THE MOCKINGBIRD

RANDALL JARRELL

Look one way and the sun is going down,
Look the other and the moon is rising.
The sparrow's shadow's longer than the lawn.
The bats squeak: "Night is here"; the birds cheep:
   "Day is gone."
On the willow's highest branch, monopolizing
Day and night, cheeping, squeaking, soaring,
The mockingbird is imitating life.

All day the mockingbird has owned the yard.
As light first woke the world, the sparrows trooped
Onto the seedy lawn: the mockingbird
Chased them off shrieking. Hour by hour, fighting hard
To make the world his own, he swooped
On thrushes, thrashers, jays, and chickadees—
At noon he drove away a big black cat.

Now, in the moonlight, he sits here and sings.
A thrush is singing, then a thrasher, then a jay—
Then, all at once, a cat begins meowing.
A mockingbird can sound like anything.
He imitates the world he drove away
So well that for a minute, in the moonlight,
Which one's the mockingbird? which one's the world?

# A NARROW FELLOW IN THE GRASS

EMILY DICKINSON

A narrow fellow in the grass
Occasionally rides;
You may have met him,—did you not?
His notice sudden is.

The grass divides as with a comb,
A spotted shaft is seen;
And then it closes at your feet
And opens further on.

He likes a boggy acre,
A floor too cool for corn.
Yet when a child, and barefoot,
I more than once, at morn,

Have passed, I thought, a whip-lash
Unbraiding in the sun,—
When, stooping to secure it,
It wrinkled, and was gone.

Several of nature's people
I know, and they know me;
I feel for them a transport
Of cordiality;

But never met this fellow,
Attended or alone,
Without a tighter breathing,
And zero at the bone.

# THE LION

HERBERT ASQUITH

The lion walks behind his bars,
  His tawny shoulders ebb and flow,
With swaying flank and lowered mane
  He pads the asphalt, proud and slow.

If he could break his rusted cage,
  How many eyes would open wide
To see him flaring through the gap,
  A lion springing in his pride!

But now he walks with silent tread,
  Swinging and turning in his den,
He yawns, and blinks his golden eyes
  Above the prying sons of men.


# GILA MONSTER

HARRY BEHN

His black tongue flickers
Tasting night.
Where are the frightened quail?
Where are the blue frogs who sing
After rain?

# DEER

HARRY BEHN

Proud in a cloud of sun
Stands deer,
His head held high
As petals fall
Over his quivering flanks.

Under a tree
Brighter than sun
Stands deer
Rubbing moss
From his polished weapons.

# DRAGONFLY

HARRY BEHN

His small feet
Pin him
To a tule reed.

Over the water
His wings pin him
Motionless in the air.

"Green, how much I want you green."

"Verde que te quiero verde."

FEDERICO GARCÍA LORCA

# THE MINIMAL

THEODORE ROETHKE

I study the lives on a leaf: the little
Sleepers, numb nudgers in cold dimensions,
Beetles in caves, newts, stone-deaf fishes,
Lice tethered to long limp subterranean weeds,
Squirmers in bogs,
And bacterial creepers
Wriggling through wounds
Like elvers in ponds,
Their wan mouths kissing the warm sutures,
Cleaning and caressing,
Creeping and healing.

# THE COMING STAR

JUAN RAMÓN JIMÉNEZ
*Translated by H. R. Hays*

The star is in the orange tree.
Let us see who can capture it!

Come quickly with pearls,
Fetch nets made of silk!

The star is on the roof.
Let us see who can capture it!*

What an odor of springtime
From its flask of eternal life!

The star is in all eyes.
Let us see who can capture it!

In the air, in the grass,
Take care, do not lose it!

The star is in love!
Let us see who can capture it!

*Translation of stanza by editor*

# LA ESTRELLA VENIDA

JUAN RAMÓN JIMÉNEZ

En el naranjo está la estrella.
¡A ver quién puede cojerla!

¡Pronto, venid con las perlas,
traed las redes de seda!

En el tejado está la estrella.
¡A ver quién puede cojerla!

¡O, qué olor a primavera
su pomo de luz eterna!

En los ojos está la estrella.
¡A ver quién puede cojerla

¡Por el aire, por la yerba!
¡Cuidado, que no se pierda!

¡En el amor está la estrella!
¡A ver quién puede cojerla!

# THE PRAYER OF THE BUTTERFLY

CARMEN BERNOS DE GASZTOLD

*Translated by Rumer Godden*

Lord!
Where was I?
Oh yes! This flower, this sun,
thank You! Your world is beautiful!
This scent of roses . . .
Where was I?
A drop of dew
rolls to sparkle in a lily's heart.
I have to go . . .
Where? I do not know!
The wind has painted fancies
on my wings.
Fancies . . .
Where was I?
Oh yes! Lord,
I had something to tell you:

                        Amen

# PRIÈRE DU PAPILLON

CARMEN BERNOS DE GASZTOLD

Seigneur!
Où en étais-je?
Ah! oui, cette fleur, ce soleil,
merci! Votre création est belle!
Ce parfum de rose . . .
Où en étais-je?
Une goutte de rosée
roule des feux de joie au cœur d'un lis.
Je devais aller . . .
Je ne sais plus!
Le vent a peint ses fantaisies
sur mes ailes.
Des fantaisies . . .
Où en étais-je?
Ah! oui, Seigneur,
j'avais quelque chose à Vous dire:
     Ainsi soit-il!

# THE CAT AND THE MOON

W. B. YEATS

The cat went here and there
And the moon spun round like a top,
And the nearest kin of the moon,
The creeping cat, looked up.
Black Minnaloushe stared at the moon,
For, wander and wail as he would,
The pure cold light in the sky
Troubled his animal blood.
Minnaloushe runs in the grass
Lifting his delicate feet.
Do you dance, Minnaloushe, do you dance?
When two close kindred meet,
What better than call a dance?
Maybe the moon may learn,
Tired of that courtly fashion,
A new dance turn.
Minnaloushe creeps through the grass
From moonlit place to place,
The sacred moon overhead
Has taken a new phase.
Does Minnaloushe know that his pupils
Will pass from change to change,
And that from round to crescent,
From crescent to round they range?
Minnaloushe creeps through the grass
Alone, important and wise,
And lifts to the changing moon
His changing eyes.

# LONELINESS

HASHIN

*Translated by Harold G. Henderson*

No sky at all;
　　no earth at all—and still
　　　　the snowflakes fall. . . .

天も地もなしに雪の降りしきり。
芭臣

# WINTER SONG

JUAN RAMÓN JIMÉNEZ
*Translated by H. R. Hays*

Singing. Singing.
Where are the birds that are singing?

It has rained. And still the branches
Have no new leaves. Singing. Birds
Are singing. Where are the birds
That are singing?

I have no birds in cages.
There are no children who sell them. Singing.
The valley is far away. Nothing . . .

I do not know where the birds are
That are singing—singing, singing—
The birds that are singing.

# CANCIÓN DE INVIERNO

JUAN RAMÓN JIMÉNEZ

Cantan. Cantan.
¿Dónde cantan los pájaros que cantan?
Ha llovido. Aún las ramas
están sin hojas nuevas. Cantan. Cantan
los pájaros. ¿En dónde cantan
los pájaros que cantan?
No tengo pájaros en jaulas.
No hay niños que los vendan. Cantan.
El valle está muy lejos. Nada . . .
Yo no sé dónde cantan
los pájaros—cantan, cantan—,
los pájaros que cantan.

# STARS

CARL SANDBURG

The stars are too many to count.
The stars make sixes and sevens.
The stars tell nothing—and everything.
The stars look scattered.
Stars are so far away they never speak
  when spoken to.

GERARD  MANLEY  HOPKINS

The stars were packed so close that night
  They seemed to press and stare
And gather in like hurdles bright
  The liberties of air.

# HALF MOON

FEDERICO GARCÍA LORCA

*Translated by W. S. Merwin*

The moon goes over the water.
How tranquil the sky is!
She goes scything slowly
the old shimmer from the river;
meanwhile a young frog
takes her for a little mirror.


# MEDIA LUNA

FEDERICO GARCÍA LORCA

La luna va por el agua.
¡Cómo está el cielo tranquilo!
Va segando lentamente
el temblor viejo del río
mientras que una rana joven
la toma por espejito.

JAMES JOYCE

All day I hear the noise of waters
    Making moan,
Sad as the sea-bird is, when going
    Forth alone,
He hears the winds cry to the waters'
    Monotone.

The grey winds, the cold winds are blowing
    Where I go.
I hear the noise of many waters
    Far below.
All day, all night, I hear them flowing
    To and fro.

## THE BRAVE MAN

WALLACE STEVENS

The sun, that brave man,
Comes through boughs that lie in wait,
That brave man.

Green and gloomy eyes
In dark forms of the grass
Run away.

The good stars,
Pale helms and spiky spurs,
Run away.

Fears of my bed,
Fears of life and fears of death,
Run away.

That brave man comes up
From below and walks without meditation,
That brave man.

# WITH THE ROSES

JUAN RAMÓN JIMÉNEZ
*Translated by H. R. Hays*

No, this sweet afternoon
I can not stay indoors;
This free afternoon
I must go out in the open air.

Into the laughing air,
Spreading through the trees
Thousands of loves,
Profound and waving.

The roses await me,
Bathing their flesh.
No boundaries contain me;
I will not stay indoors.

# CON LAS ROSAS

JUAN RAMÓN JIMÉNEZ

No, esta dulce tarde
no puedo quedarme;
esta tarde libre
tengo que irme al aire.

Al aire que ríe
abriendo los árboles,
amores a miles,
profundo, ondeante.

Me esperan las rosas
bañando su carne.
¡No me claves fines;
no quiero quedarme!

# WINTER

JŌSŌ
*Translated by Harold G. Henderson*

Mountains and plains,
   all are captured by snow—
      nothing remains.

野も山も雪にとられてなにもなし。 丈草

# THE WIND

JAMES STEPHENS

The wind stood up, and gave a shout;
He whistled on his fingers, and

Kicked the withered leaves about,
And thumped the branches with his hand,

And said he'll kill, and kill, and kill;
And so he will! And so he will!


# SEA CALM

LANGSTON HUGHES

How still,
How strangely still
The water is today.
It is not good
For water
To be so still that way.

" . . . music heard so deeply
That it is not heard at all, but you are the music
While the music lasts."

T. S. ELIOT

# MY VOICE

JUAN RAMÓN JIMÉNEZ
*Translated by H. R. Hays*

Sing, sing, voice of mine,
While there is something
You have not said.
You have said nothing at all.


# VOZ MÍA

JUAN RAMÓN JIMÉNEZ

¡Voz mía, canta, canta;
que mientras haya algo
que no hayas dicho tú,
tú nada has dicho!

# *From* PRAISE TO THE END!

THEODORE ROETHKE

Mips and ma the mooly moo,
The likes of him is biting who,
A cow's a care and who's a coo?—
What footie does is final.

My dearest dear my fairest fair,
Your father tossed a cat in air,
Though neither you nor I was there,—
What footie does is final.

Be large as an owl, be slick as a frog,
Be good as a goose, be big as a dog,
Be sleek as a heifer, be long as a hog,—
What footie will do will be final.

porky & porkie
sit into a moon)

blacker than dreams
are round like a spoon are
both making silence

two-made-of-one

& nothing tells anywhere
"snow will come soon" &
pretending they're birds sit

creatures of quills
(asleep who must go

things-without-wings

# ON THE BEACH AT FONTANA

JAMES JOYCE

Wind whines and whines the shingle,
The crazy pierstakes groan;
A senile sea numbers each single
Slimesilvered stone

From whining wind and colder
Grey sea I wrap him warm
And touch his trembling fineboned shoulder
And boyish arm.

Around us fear, descending
Darkness of fear above
And in my heart how deep unending
Ache of love!

# *From* THE LOST SON

THEODORE ROETHKE

The shape of a rat?
       It's bigger than that.
       It's less than a leg
       And more than a nose,
       Just under the water
       It usually goes.

Is it soft like a mouse?
Can it wrinkle its nose?
Could it come in the house
On the tips of its toes?

Take the skin of a cat
And the back of an eel,
Then roll them in grease,—
That's the way it would feel.

It's sleek as an otter
With wide webby toes
Just under the water
It usually goes.

# EASTER SUNDAY

SEDULIUS SCOTTUS

*Translated by Helen Waddell*

Last night did Christ the Sun rise from the dark,
  The mystic harvest of the fields of God,
And now the little wandering tribes of bees
  Are brawling in the scarlet flowers abroad.
The winds are soft with birdsong; all night long
  Darkling the nightingale her descant told,
And now inside church doors the happy folk
  The Alleluia chant a hundredfold.
O father of thy folk, be thine by right
The Easter joy, the threshold of the light.


# CARMEN PASCHALE

SEDULIUS SCOTTUS

Surrexit Christus sol verus vespere noctis,
  surgit et hinc domini mystica messis agri.
nun vaga puniceis apium plebs laeta labore
  floribus instrepitans poblite mella legit.
nunc variae volucres permulcent aethera cantu,
  temperat et pernox nunc philomela melos.
nunc chorus ecclesiae cantat per cantica Sion,
  alleluia suis centuplicatque tonis.
Tado, pater patriae, caelestis gaudia paschae
  percipias meritis limina lucis: ave.

# BEETHOVEN'S DEATH MASK

STEPHEN SPENDER

I imagine him still with heavy brow.
Huge, black, with bent head and falling hair,
He ploughs the landscape. His face
Is this hanging mask transfigured,
This mask of death which the white lights make stare.

I see the thick hands clasped; the scare-crow coat;
The light strike upwards at the holes for eyes;
The beast squat in that mouth, whose opening is
The hollow opening of an organ pipe:
There the wind sings and the harsh longing cries.

He moves across my vision like a ship.
What else is iron but he? The fields divide
And, heaving, are changing waters of the sea.
He is prisoned, masked, shut off from being.
Life, like a fountain, he sees leap—outside.

Yet, in that head there twists the roaring cloud
And coils, as in a shell, the roaring wave.
The damp leaves whisper; bending to the rain
The April rises in him, chokes his lungs
And climbs the torturing passage of his brain.

Then the drums move away, the Distance shows:
Now cloud-hid peaks are bared; the mystic One
Horizons haze, as the blue incense, heaven.
Peace, peace. . . . Then splitting skull and dream, there come
Blotting our lights, the Trumpeter, the sun.

# IN THE EVENING

G. K. CHESTERTON

It is the little brown hour of twilight.
I pause between two dark houses,
   For there is a song in my heart.
If I could sing at this moment what I wish to sing,
The nations would crown me,
   If I were dumb ever afterwards.
For I am sure it would be the greatest song in the world,
And the song every one has been trying to sing
     Just now!
   But it will not come out.


# *From* THE WRECK OF THE DEUTSCHLAND

GERARD MANLEY HOPKINS

14

    She drove in the dark to leeward,
    She struck—not a reef or a rock
  But the combs of a smother of sand: night drew her
    Dead to the Kentish Knock;
And she beat the bank down with her bows and the ride of
    her keel:
The breakers rolled on her beam with ruinous shock;
   And canvas and compass, the whorl and the sheel
Idle for ever to waft her or wind her with, these she endured.

# THE DREAM

HARRY BEHN

One night I dreamed
I was lost in a cave,
A cave that was empty
And dark and cool,
And down into nothing
I dropped a stone
And it fell like a star
Far and alone,
And a sigh arose
The sigh of a wave
Rippling the heart
Of a sunless pool.

And after a while
In my dream I dreamed
I climbed a sky
That was high and steep
And still as a mountain
Without a cave,
As still as water
Without a wave,
And on that hill
Of the sun it seemed
That all sad sounds
In the world fell asleep.

# BALLAD OF THE LITTLE SQUARE

FEDERICO GARCÍA LORCA
*Translated by Stephen Spender and J. L. Gili*

The children sing
in the quiet night;
clear stream,
serene fountain!

*The Children*
What joy does your divine
heart celebrate?

*Myself*
A clanging of bells
lost in the mist.

*The Children*
You leave us singing
in the little square.
Clear stream,
serene fountain!

What signs of spring
do you hold in your hand?

*Myself*
A rose of blood
and a white lily.

*The Children*
Dip them in the water
of the antique song.
Clear stream,
serene fountain!

What do you feel in your mouth
scarlet and thirsting?

*Myself*
The savour of the bones
of my great skull.

*The Children*
Drink the tranquil water
of the antique song.
Clear stream,
serene fountain!

Why do you go so far
from the little square?

*Myself*
I go in search of magicians
and of princesses!

*The Children*
Who showed you the path
of the poets?

*Myself*
The fountain and the stream
of the antique song.

*The Children*
Do you go far, very far
from the sea and the earth?

*Myself*
My heart of silk
is filled with lights,
with lost bells,
with lilies and bees.
I will go very far,
farther than those hills,
farther than the seas,
close to the stars,
to beg Christ the Lord
to give back the soul I had
of old, when I was a child,
ripened with legends,
with a feathered cap
and a wooden sword.

*The Children*
You leave us singing
in the little square,
clear stream,
serene fountain!

The enormous pupils
of the parched fronds
injured by the wind,
the dead leaves weep.

# BALADA DE LA PLACETA

FEDERICO GARCÍA LORCA

Cantan los niños
en la noche quieta;
¡arroyo claro,
fuente serena!

*Los Niños*
¿Qué tiene tu divino
corazón en fiesta?

*Yo*
Un doblar de campanas
perdidas en la niebla.

*Los Niños*
Ya nos dejas cantando
en la plazuela.
¡Arroyo claro,
fuente serena!

¿Qué tienes en tus manos
de primavera?

*Yo*
Una rosa de sangre
y una azucena.

*Los Niños*
Mójalas en el agua
de la canción añeja.
¡Arroyo claro,
fuente serena!

¿Qúe sientes en tu boca
roja y sedienta?

*Yo*
El sabor de los huesos
de mi gran calavera.

*Los Niños*
Bebe el agua tranquila
de la canción añeja.
¡Arroyo claro,
fuente serena!

¿Por qué te vas tan lejos
de la plazuela?

*Yo*
¡Voy en busca de magos
y de princesas!

*Los Niños*
¿Quién te enseñó el camino
de los poetas?

*Yo*
La fuente y el arroyo
de la canción añeja.

*Los Niños*
¿Te vas lejos, muy lejos
del mar y de la tierra?

*Yo*
Se ha llenado de luces
mi corazón de seda,
de campanas perdidas,
de lirios y de abejas.
Y yo me iré muy lejos,
más allá de esas sierras,
más allá de los mares,
cerca de las estrellas,
para perdirle a Cristo
Señor que me devuelva
mi alma antigua de niño,
madura de leyendas,
con el gorro de plumas
y el sable de madera.

*Los Niños*
Ya nos dejas cantando
en la plazuela,
¡arroyo claro,
fuente serena!

Las pupilas enormes
de las frondas resecas,
heridas por el viento,
lloran has hojas muertas.

"I hear an army charging upon the land"

JAMES JOYCE

# BALLAD OF THE SOLDIER

BERTOLT BRECHT

*Translated by H. R. Hays*

The trigger will shoot and the dagger will strike,
If you wade in the water 'twill freeze you.
Watch out for the ice, keep out if you're wise,
Said the goodwife to the soldier.

But the soldier boy with his weapons in place
Harked to the drumming and laughed in her face.
For bugles and drums never hurt you.
From the north to the south he'll march all his life
And his fingers were made just to handle a knife,
The soldiers they said to the goodwife.

Oh bitter you'll mourn the counsel you scorn
When you turn a deaf ear to your elders.
In God's name here abide, there's danger outside,
Said the goodwife to the soldier.

But the soldier boy, with his pistol and sword,
Laughed aloud at her words and crossed over the ford,
For how could the cold water hurt him?
When the moon glimmers white on the crest of the knoll,
You shall see us again. Now pray for his soul,
The soldiers they said to the goodwife.

You are gone like smoke. And the heat is gone, too.
For your glory can never warm us.
How quick the smoke goes! Then God preserve you,
Said the goodwife of the soldier.

And the soldier boy with his pistol and sword
Sank down with the spear and was lost in the ford
And he waded in water that froze him.
And cool on the crest the moon shone white
But the soldier and ice whirled away in the night
And then what did they say to the goodwife?

He is gone like smoke and the heat is gone, too
And his deeds will never warm her.
Oh bitter to mourn women's counsel you scorn,
Said the goodwife to the soldier.


## DIE BALLADE VON DEM SOLDATEN

BERTOLT BRECHT

Das Schiessgewehr schiesst und das Spiessmesser spiesst
Und das Wasser frisst auf, die drin waten.
Was könnt ihr gegen Eis? Bleibt weg, 's ist nicht weis'!
Sagte das Weib zum Soldaten.

Doch der Soldat mit der Kugel im Lauf
Hörte die Trommel und lachte darauf
Marschieren kann nimmermehr schaden!
Hinab nach dem Süden, nach dem Norden hinauf
Und das Messer fängt er mit Händen auf!
Sagten zum Weib die Soldaten.

Ach, bitter bereut, wer des Weisen Rat scheut
Und vom Alter sich nicht lässt beraten!
Ach, zu hoch nicht hinaus, es geht übel aus!
Sagte das Weib zum Soldaten.

Doch der Soldat mit dem Messer im Gurt
Lacht ihr kalt ins Gesicht und ging über die Furt
Was konnte das Wasser ihm schaden?
Wenn weiss der Mond überm Mongefluss steht
Kommen wir wieder; nimm's auf ins Gebet!
Sagten zum Weib die Soldaten.

Ihr vergeht wie der Rauch, und die Wärme geht auch
Und uns wärmen nicht eure Taten!
Ach, wie schnell geht der Rauch! Gott, behüte ihn auch!
Sagte das Weib vom Soldaten.

Und der Soldat mit dem Messer am Gurt
Sank hin mit dem Speer, und mit riss ihn die Furt
Und das Wasser frauss auf, die drin waten.
Kühl stand der Mond überm Mongefluss weiss
Doch der Soldat trieb hinab mit dem Eis
Und was sagten dem Weib die Soldaten?

Er verging wie der Rauch, und die Wärme ging auch
Und es wärmten sie nicht seine Taten.
Ach bitter bereut, wer des Weibes Rat scheut!
Sagte das Weib zum Soldaten.

# From TO HIS FRIEND, WEI, . . .

LI PO

*Translated by Shigeyoshi Obata*

Summers and winters had come and gone—how many times?—
And suddenly the empire was wrecked.
The imperial army met the barbarian foe,
The dust of the battlefield darkened sky and sea,
And the sun and moon were no longer bright
While the wind of death shook the grass and trees.
And the white bones were piled up in hills—
Ah, what had they done—the innocent people?

贈江夏韋太守良宰。

榮枯異炎涼。炎涼幾度改。九土中橫潰。漢甲連胡兵。
沙塵暗雲海。草木搖殺氣。星辰無光彩。白骨成丘山。
蒼生竟何罪。

李白

235

# BIVOUAC ON A MOUNTAIN SIDE

WALT WHITMAN

I see before me now a traveling army halting,
Below a fertile valley spread, with barns and the orchards of
    summer,
Behind, the terraced sides of a mountain, abrupt, in places
    rising high,
Broken, with rocks, with clinging cedars, with tall shapes
    dingily seen,
The numerous camp-fires scatter'd near and far, some away
    up on the mountain,
The shadowy forms of men and horses, looming, large-sized,
    flickering,
And over all the sky—the sky! far, far out of reach, studded,
    breaking out, the eternal stars.


# FAST RODE THE KNIGHT

STEPHEN CRANE

Fast rode the knight
With spurs, hot and reeking,
Ever waving an eager sword,
"To save my lady!"
Fast rode the knight,
And leaped from saddle to war.
Men of steel flickered and gleamed
Like riot of silver lights,

And the gold of the knight's good banner
Still waved on the castle wall.

   .   .   .

A horse,
Blowing, staggering, bloody thing,
Forgotten at foot of castle wall.
A horse
Dead at foot of castle wall.

## From A FEW THINGS EXPLAINED

PABLO NERUDA

*Translated by Ben Belitt*

I'll tell you how matters stand with me.

I lived for a time in suburban
Madrid, with its bells
and its clocks and its trees.

The face of Castile
could be seen from that place, parched,
like an ocean of leather.

      People spoke of my house
as "the house with the flowers"; it exploded
geraniums: such a beautiful
house, with the
dogs and the small fry.

                    Remember, Raul?
Remember it, Rafael?
                    Federico, under the ground
there, remember it?
Can you remember my house with the balconies where
June drowned the dazzle of flowers in your teeth?

                    Ah, brother, my brother!

All
the voices were generous, the salt of the market place,
convocations of shimmering bread,
the stalls of suburban Argüelles with its statue
as wan as an inkwell in the sheen of the hake:
oil swam in the spoons,
a wild pandemonium
of fingers and feet overflowing the streets,
meters and liters, all the avid
quintessence of living,
                    fish packed in the stands,
a contexture of roofs in the chill of the sun
where the arrowpoints faltered;
potatoes, inflamed and fastidious ivory,
tomatoes again and again to the sea.

Till one morning everything blazed:
one morning bonfires
sprang out of earth
and devoured all the living;
since then, only fire,
since then, the blood and the gunpowder,
ever since then.

# *From* EXPLICIO ALGUNAS COSAS

PABLO NERUDA

Os voy a contar todo lo que me pasa.

Yo vivía en un barrio
de Madrid, con campanas,
con relojes, con árboles.

Desde allí se veía
el rostro seco de Castilla
come un océano de cuero.

               Mi casa era llamada
la casa de las flores, porque por todas partes
estallaban geranios: era
una bella casa
con perros y chiquillos.
               Raúl, te acuerdas?
Te acuerdas, Rafael?
               Federico, te acuerdas
debajo de la tierra,
te acuerdas de mi casa con balcones en donde
la luz de junio ahogaba flores en tu boca?

               Hermano, hermano!

Todo
era grandes voces, sal de mercaderías,
aglomeraciones de pan palpitante,
mercados de mi barrio de Argüelles con su estatua
como un tintero pálido entre las merluzas:
el aceite llegaba a las cucharas,
un profundo latido
de pies y manos llenaba las calles,

metros, litros, esencia
aguda de la vida,
                    pescados hacinados,
contextura de techos con sol frío en el cual
la flecha se fatiga,
delirante marfil fino de las patatas,
tomates repetidos hasta el mar.

Y una mañana todo estaba ardiendo
y una mañana las hogueras
salían de la tierra
devorando seres,
y desde entonces fuego,
pólvora desde entonces,
y desde entonces sangre.

# THE NEFARIOUS WAR

LI PO

*Translated by Shigeyoshi Obata*

Last year we fought by the head-stream of the Sang-kan,
This year we are fighting on the Tsung-ho road.
We have washed our armor in the waves of the Chiao-chi lake,
We have pastured our horses on Tien-shan's snowy slopes.
The long, long war goes on ten thousand miles from home,
Our three armies are worn and grown old.

The barbarian does man-slaughter for plowing;
On his yellow sand-plains nothing has been seen but blanched
     skulls and bones.
Where the Chin emperor built the walls against the Tartars,
There the defenders of Han are burning beacon fires.
The beacon fires burn and never go out,
There is no end to war!—

In the battlefield men grapple each other and die;
The horses of the vanquished utter lamentable cries to heaven,
While ravens and kites peck at human entrails,
Carry them up in their flight, and hang them on the branches of
     dead trees.
So, men are scattered and smeared over the desert grass,
And the generals have accomplished nothing.

Oh, nefarious war! I see why arms
Were so seldom used by the benign sovereigns.

戰城南

去年戰桑乾源。今年戰蔥河道。洗兵條支海上波。放馬天山雪中草。
萬里長征戰。三軍盡衰老。匈奴以殺戮爲耕作。古來唯見白骨
黃沙田。秦家築城備胡處。漢家還有烽火燃。烽火然不息。征
戰無已時。野戰格鬥死。敗馬號鳴向天悲。烏鳶啄人腸。銜
飛上桂枯樹枝。士卒塗草莽。將軍爾爲。乃知兵者是凶器。聖
人不得已而用之。

李白

242

# AFTER THE SALVO

HERBERT ASQUITH

Up and down, up and down,
They go, the gray rat, and the brown.
The telegraph lines are tangled hair,
Motionless on the sullen air;
An engine has fallen on its back,
With crazy wheels, on a twisted track;
All ground to dust is the little town;
Up and down, up and down
They go, the gray rat, and the brown.
A skull, torn out of the graves nearby,
Gapes in the grass. A butterfly
In azure iridescence new,
Floats into the world, across the dew;
Between the flow'rs. Have we lost our way,
Or are we toys of a god at play,
Who do these things on a young Spring day?

Where the salvo fell, on a splintered ledge
Of ruin, at the crater's edge,
A poppy lives: and young, and fair,
The dewdrops hang on the spider's stair,
With every rainbow still unhurt
From leaflet unto leaflet girt.
Man's house is crushed; the spider's lives:
Inscrutably He takes, and gives,
Who guards not any temple here,
Save the temple of the gossamer.

Up and down, up and down
They go, the gray rat and the brown:
A pistol cracks: they too are dead.

The nightwind rustles overhead.


# DEAD COW FARM

ROBERT GRAVES

An ancient saga tells us how
In the beginning the First Cow
(For nothing living yet had birth
But Elemental Cow on earth)
Began to lick cold stones and mud:
Under her warm tongue flesh and blood
Blossomed, a miracle to believe:
And so was Adam born, and Eve.
Here now is chaos once again,
Primeval mud, cold stones and rain.
Here flesh decays and blood drips red,
And the Cow's dead, the old Cow's dead.

"... a newer, mightier world, varied world"

WALT WHITMAN

# KID STUFF

## December, 1942

FRANK HORNE

The wise guys
tell me
that Christmas
is Kid Stuff . . .
Maybe they've got
something there—
Two thousand years ago
three wise guys
chased a star
across a continent
to bring
frankincense and myrrh
to a Kid
born in a manger
with an idea in his head . . .

And as the bombs
crash
all over the world
today
the real wise guys
know
that we've all
got to go chasing stars
again
in the hope
that we can get back
some of that
Kid Stuff
born two thousand years ago.

# EUCLID

VACHEL LINDSAY

Old Euclid drew a circle
On a sand-beach long ago.
He bounded and enclosed it
With angles thus and so.
His set of solemn graybeards
Nodded and argued much
Of arc and of circumference,
Diameter and such.
A silent child stood by them
From morning until noon
Because they drew such charming
Round pictures of the moon.

# LINCOLN MONUMENT: WASHINGTON

LANGSTON HUGHES

Let's go see old Abe
Sitting in the marble and the moonlight,
Sitting lonely in the marble and the moonlight,
Quiet for ten thousand centuries, old Abe.
Quiet for a million, million years.

Quiet—

And yet a voice forever
Against the
Timeless walls
Of time—
Old Abe.

# THEN AS NOW

WALTER DE LA MARE

Then as Now; and Now as Then,
Spins on this World of Men.
White—Black—Yellow—Red:
They wake, work, eat, play, go to bed.
Black—Yellow—Red—White:
They talk, laugh, weep, dance, morn to night.
Yellow—Red—White—Black:
Sun shines, moon rides, clouds come back.
Red—White—Black—Yellow:
Count your hardest, who could tell o'
The myriads that have come and gone,
Stayed their stay this earth upon,
And vanished then, their labour done?
Sands of the wilderness, stars in heaven,
Solomon could not sum them even:
Then as Now; Now as Then
Still spins on this World of Men.

# THE MOTION OF THE EARTH

NORMAN NICHOLSON

A day with sky so wide,
So stripped of cloud, so scrubbed, so vacuumed free
Of dust, that you can see
The earth-line as a curve, can watch the blue
Wrap over the edge, looping round and under,
Making you wonder
Whether the dark has anywhere left to hide.
But the world is slipping away; the polished sky
Gives nothing to grip on; clicked from the knuckle
The marble rolls along the gutter of time—
Earth, star and galaxy
Shifting their place in space.
Noon, sunset, clouds, the equably varying weather,
The diffused light, the illusion of blue,
Conceal each hour a different constellation.
All things are new
Over the sun, but we,
Our eyes on our shoes, go staring
At the asphalt, the gravel, the grass at the roadside, the door-
step, the doodles of snails, the crochet of mortar and lime,
Seeking the seeming familiar, though every stride
Takes us a thousand miles from where we were before.

ROBERT FROST

But outer Space,
At least this far,
For all the fuss
Of the popul*ace*,
Stays more popu*lar*
Than popul*ous*.


*From* THE LIGHTS IN THE SKY ARE STARS

KENNETH REXROTH

Believe in Orion. Believe
In the night, the moon, the crowded
Earth. Believe in Christmas and
Birthdays and Easter rabbits.
Believe in all those fugitive
Compounds of nature, all doomed
To waste away and go out.
Always be true to these things.
They are all there is.

# OUTWARD

LOUIS SIMPSON

The staff slips from the hand
Hissing and swims on the polished floor.
It glides away to the desert.

It floats like a bird or lily
On the waves, to the ones who are arriving.
And if no god arrives,

Then everything yearns outward.
The honeycomb cell brims over
And the atom is broken in light.

Machines have made their god. They walk or fly.
The towers bend like Magi, mountains weep,
Needles go mad, and metal sheds a tear.

*

The astronaut is lifted
Away from the world, and drifts.
How easy it is to be there!

How easy to be anyone, anything but oneself!
The metal of the plane is breathing;
Sinuously it swims through the stars.

# BROOKLYN BRIDGE

VLADIMIR MAYAKOVSKY

*Translated by Max Hayward and George Reavey*

Give, Coolidge,
a shout of joy!
I too will spare no words
                  about good things.
Blush
      at my praise,
                go red as our flag,
however
       united-states
              -of
-america you may be.
As a crazed believer
                enters
                   a church,
retreats
      into a monastery cell,
                   austere and plain;
so I,
      in graying evening
               haze,
humbly set foot
           on Brooklyn Bridge.
As a conqueror presses
             into a city
                all shattered,
on cannon with muzzles
           craning high as a giraffe—
so, drunk with glory,

                    eager to live,
I clamber,
            in pride,
                        upon Brooklyn Bridge.
As a foolish painter
                    plunges his eye,
sharp and loving,
                into a museum madonna,
so I,
        from the near skies
                        bestrewn with stars,
gaze
        at New York
                    through the Brooklyn Bridge.
New York
            heavy and stifling
                            till night,
has forgotten
                its hardships
                            and height;
and only
            the household ghosts
ascend
            in the lucid glow of its windows.
Here
        the elevateds
                    drone softly.
And only
            their gentle
                        droning
tell us:
        here trains
                    are crawling and rattling
like dishes

255

being cleared into a cupboard.
While
        a shopkeeper fetched sugar
from a mill
            that seemed to project
                            out of the water—
the masts
            passing under the bridge
looked
        no larger than pins.
I am proud
            of just this
                    mile of steel;
upon it,
        my visions come to life, erect—
here's a fight
                for construction
                                instead of style,
an austere disposition
                    of bolts
                        and steel.
If
    the end of the world
                    befall—
and chaos
        smash our planet
                        to bits,
and what remains
                will be
                        this
bridge, rearing above the dust of destruction;
then,
        as huge ancient lizards
                        are rebuilt

from bones
          finer than needles,
                    to tower in museums,
so,
     from this bridge,
                    a geologist of the centuries
will succeed
          in recreating
                    our contemporary world.
He will say:
          —Yonder paw
                    of steel
once joined
          the seas and the prairies;
from this spot,
                    Europe
                         rushed to the West,
scattering
          to the wind
                    Indian feathers.
This rib
          reminds us
                    of a machine—
just imagine,
          would there be hands enough,
after planting
          a steel foot
                    in Manhattan,
to yank
          Brooklyn to oneself
                    by the lip?
By the cables
          of electric strands,

257

I recognize
          the era succeeding
                    the steam age—
here
     men
          had ranted
                    on radio.
Here
     men
          had ascended
                    in planes.
For some,
          life
               here
                    had no worries;
for others,
          it was a prolonged
                    and hungry howl.
From this spot,
                    jobless men
lept
     headlong
               into the Hudson.*
Now
     my canvas
               is unobstructed
as it stretches on cables of string
                    to the feet of the stars.
I see:
     here
          stood Mayakovsky,

---

* Mayakovsky mistook the East River for the Hudson.

stood,

        composing verse, syllable by syllable.

I stare

        as an Eskimo gapes at a train,

I seize on it

           as a tick fastens to an ear.

Brooklyn Bridge—

yes . . .

        That's quite a thing!

(1925)

## БРУКЛИНСКИЙ МОСТ

ВЛАДИМИР МАЯКОВСКИЙ

Издай, Кулидж,

радостный клич!

На хорошее

        и мне не жалко слов.

От похвал

      краснея,

           как Флага нашего материйка,

хоть вы

     и разъюнайтед стетс

             оф

Америка.

Как в церковь

      идет

          помешавшийся верующий,

как в скит

удаляется,
        строг и прост,—
так я
   в вечерней
        сереющей мерещи
вхожу,
     смиренный, на Бруклинский мост.
Как в город
     в сломанный
         прет победитель
на пушках—жерлом
        жирафу под рост—
так, пьяный славой,
      так жить в аппетите,
влезаю,
    гордый,
        на Бруклинский мост.
Как глупый художник
          в мадонну музея
вонзает глаз свой,
        влюблен и остр,
так я,
    с поднебесья,
        в звезды усеян,
смотрю
     на Нью-Йорк
        сквозь Бруклинский мост.
Нью-Йорк
     до вечера тяжек
        и душен,
забыл,
    что тяжко ему
       и высоко,
и только одни

домовьи души

встают

в прозрачном свечении окон.

Здесь

еле зудит

элевейтеров зуд.

И только

по этому

тихому зуду

поймешь—

поезда

с дребезжаньем ползут,

как будто

в буфет убирают посуду.

Когда ж,

казалось, с под речки начатой

развозит

с фабрики

сахар лавочник,—

то

под мостом проходящие мачты

размером

не больше размеров булавочных.

Я горд

вот этой

стальною милей,

живьем в ней

мои видения встали—

борьба

за конструкции

вместо стилей,

расчет суровый

гаек

и стали.

Если
    придет
        окончание света—
планету
      хаос
         разделает влоск,
и только
      один останется
            этот
над пылью гибели вздыбленный мост,
то,
    как из косточек,
         тоньше иголок,
тучнеют
      в музеях стоящие
           ящеры,
так
    с этим мостом
        столетий геолог
сумел
    воссоздать бы
        дни настоящие.
Он скажет:
      —Вот эта
        стальная лапа
соединяла
    моря и прерии,
отсюда
      Европа
        рвалась на Запад,
пустив
    по ветру
      индейские перья.

Напомнит
        машину
             ребро вот это—
сообразите,
        хватит рук ли,
чтоб, став,
        стальной ногой
             на Мангетен,
к себе
     за губу
          притягивать Бруклин?
По проводам
        злектрической пряди—
я знаю—
       зпоха
          после пара—
здесь
    люди
       уже
          орали по радио,
здесь
    люди
       уже
          взлетали по аэро.
Здесь
    жизнь
       была
          одним—беззаботная,
другим—
      голодный
         протяжный вой.

Отсюда
        безработные
в Гудзон
            кидались
                        вниз головой.
И дальше
        картина моя
                 без загвоздки
по струнам-канатам,
                аж звездам к ногам.
Я вижу—
        здесь
               стоял Маяковский,
стоял
        и стихи слагал по слогам.—
Смотрю,
          как в поезд глядит эскимос,
впиваюсь,
          как в ухо впивается клещ.
Бруклинский мост—
да . . .
        Это вещь!

## *From* THE SOUND TRACK
### From *Land of the Free*

ARCHIBALD MacLEISH

We tell our freedom backward by the land

We tell our past by the gravestones and the apple trees

We wonder whether the great American dream
Was the singing of locusts out of the grass to the west and the
West is behind us now:

The west wind's away from us

We wonder if the liberty is done:
The dreaming is finished

We can't say

We aren't sure

Or if there's something different men can dream

Or if there's something different men can mean by
Liberty. . . .

Or if there's liberty a man can mean that's
Men: not land

We wonder

We don't know

We're asking

# YOUTH

LANGSTON HUGHES

We have tomorrow
Bright before us
Like a flame.

Yesterday
A night-gone thing,
A sun-down name.

And dawn today
Broad arch above the road we came.

We march!

# "GO TO THE SHINE THAT'S ON A TREE"

RICHARD EBERHART

Go to the shine that's on a tree
When dawn has laved with liquid light
With luminous light the nighted tree
And take that glory without fright.

Go to the song that's in a bird
When he has seen the glistening tree,
That glorious tree the bird has heard
Give praise for its felicity.

Then go to the earth and touch it keen,
Be tree and bird, be wide aware
Be wild aware of light unseen,
And unheard song along the air.

# ON LOOKING UP BY CHANCE AT
# THE CONSTELLATIONS

ROBERT FROST

You'll wait a long, long time for anything much
To happen in heaven beyond the floats of cloud
And the Northern Lights that run like tingling nerves.
The sun and moon get crossed, but they never touch,
Nor strike out fire from each other, nor crash out loud.
The planets seem to interfere in their curves,
But nothing ever happens, no harm is done.
We may as well go patiently on with our life,
And look elsewhere than to stars and moon and sun
For the shocks and changes we need to keep us sane.
It is true the longest drouth will end in rain,
The longest peace in China will end in strife.
Still it wouldn't reward the watcher to stay awake
In hopes of seeing the calm of heaven break
On his particular time and personal sight.
That calm seems certainly safe to last tonight.

# INDEX OF TITLES

*Both original language and English translation

# INDEX OF FIRST LINES

# INDEX OF AUTHORS

# INDEX OF TRANSLATORS